The Mini Manual of

Calorie Counting

First published by Parragon in 2010

Parragon

Queen Street House

4 Queen Street

Bath BA1 1HE, UK

Page layout by Stonecastle Graphics

ISBN 978-1-4075-9356-2

Printed in China

The Mini Manual of

Calorie Counting

Bath · New York · Singapore · Hong Kong · Cologne · Delhi · Melbourne

CONTENTS

INTRODUCTION

The aim of this book is to give you a greater understanding of food. We are all familiar with the term "calories" and have some understanding of fat and its role in health. Because we eat food, we have a natural interest in it. However, we are often very confused about many issues surrounding food and diet. We are told one thing one day and, lo and behold, the next day it seems it is completely different. Who do you believe, who is telling the truth? It is all too easy to become overanxious about food, whether about becoming too fat or simply eating the wrong things.

This book begins by describing the different nutrients found in food. It gives you an idea of what these nutrients do, together with information on the amount that a healthy person needs. It then describes the important role that food plays in normal health. However, when we select food to eat, our personal preferences rather than the benefits of the nutrients tend to dictate choice. This book will help us to select certain foods because we know that they are a good source of a certain valuable nutrient.

We next learn a little more about the importance of nutrition and are guided on how to choose a balanced diet, with practical advice as to how to create a healthy diet while still keeping our enjoyment of food alive.

WHY A FAT, CARBOHYDRATE & FIBER COUNTER?

Balancing the amounts of fat, carbohydrate, and fiber we consume daily is vital to good health. Your diet should provide all the energy, protein, vitamins, and minerals you need to stay healthy and active every day, so enabling you to enjoy life to the full.

In our affluent Western society, however, it is very easy to choose a diet that is too high in fat, sugar, and salt and too low in fiber, especially as our busy lifestyles often mean that we eat takeout meals or ready-made foods. It is well known that a high-fat, high-sugar, high-salt diet may be harmful, leading to increased risk of coronary heart disease, high blood pressure, and certain forms of cancer.

Choosing to eat sensibly is clearly vital to good health. Although there are no single "good" or "bad" foods, the key to better health is to select a balanced range of nutritious foods every day, and indulge in fattening or less nutritious "treats" less often.

The Mini Manual of Calorie Counting is designed to help you achieve this. It will enable you to understand the composition of a wide range of available foods and give you the knowledge to select and balance your daily nutritional requirements and those of your family.

Dietary energy is measured in kilocalories (kcal), which comes from three major food sources: protein, fat, and carbohydrate. The daily number of calories (as they are more usually known) needed depends on your sex, age, weight, and activity level.

While protein is essential for the growth and maintenance of body tissues, most adults eat more than enough. High-fiber foods, such as bread and legumes, also provide useful amounts of protein, so achieving your daily fiber target can mean that you also obtain your protein requirements.

The A–Z food listing focuses on counting three essential nutrition elements in the foods you choose: fat, carbohydrate, and fiber. (Although fiber is not a nutrient, it has a vital role in keeping the digestive system active and healthy.)

If you follow the recommendations for your daily intake, you will also obtain the optimum protein, vitamins, and minerals essential for good health. The most useful foods are highest in carbohydrate and fiber—so aim to limit the fats and choose starchy, not sugary (low-fiber), carbohydrates.

Your diet need not meet strict daily targets. Balance too much fat one day with less the next. Overall, try to achieve a healthy diet and remember that eating should be enjoyed!

THE FOOD GUIDE PYRAMID

The food guide pyramid released by the United States Department of Agriculture (USDA) stresses activity and moderation along with a proper mix of food groups in one's diet. As part of the MyPyramid food guidance system, consumers are asked to visit the MyPyramid website for personalized nutrition information. (more info: www.MyPyramid.gov)

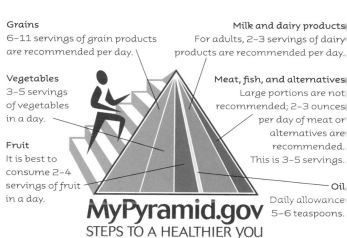

Grains
6–11 servings of grain products are recommended per day.

Vegetables
3–5 servings of vegetables in a day.

Fruit
It is best to consume 2–4 servings of fruit in a day.

Milk and dairy products
For adults, 2–3 servings of dairy products are recommended per day.

Meat, fish, and alternatives
Large portions are not recommended; 2–3 ounces per day of meat or alternatives are recommended. This is 3–5 servings.

Oil
Daily allowance 5–6 teaspoons.

FOOD GROUPS (according to the Food Guide Pyramid)

Grains Group

Cereals, breads, pastas, crackers, and rice all fall under this categorization. Grains supply food energy in the form of starch, and are also a source of protein. Whole grains contain dietary fiber, essential fatty acids, and other important nutrients. Milled grains have many nutrients removed in the milling process and thus are not as highly recommended as whole grains. Whole grains can be found especially in oatmeal, brown rice, grits, corn tortillas, and whole wheat bread.

Vegetable Group

Vegetables contain many vitamins and minerals; however, different vegetables contain different spreads, so eat a wide variety of types. For example, green vegetables typically contain vitamin A, dark orange and dark green vegetables contain vitamin C, and bushy vegetables like broccoli and related plants contain iron and calcium. Vegetables are very low in fats and calories, but cooking can often add these.

Fruit Group

This includes apples, oranges, plums, and bananas, etc. They are low in calories and fat and are a source of natural sugars, fiber, and vitamins. Fresh fruit or canned fruit packed in juice rather than syrup is recommended. The fruit food group is sometimes combined with the vegetable food group.

Milk, Yogurt, and Cheese Group

They include milk and yogurt and cheese. They are the

best source for the mineral calcium, but also provide protein, phosphorus, vitamin A, and in fortified milk, vitamin D. However, many dairy products are high in fat, and skimmed products are available as an alternative.

Meat, Poultry, Fish, Dry Beans, Eggs, and Nuts Group
Meat is a major source of protein, as well as iron, zinc, and vitamin B12. Meats, poultry, and fish include beef, chicken, pork, salmon, tuna, and shrimp, etc.

However, since many of the same nutrients found in meat can also be found in foods like eggs, dry beans, and nuts, such foods are typically placed in the same category as meats, as meat alternatives. These include tofu, products that resemble meat or fish but are made with soy, eggs, and cheeses. The meat group is one of the major compacted food groups in the food guide pyramid. Meats are often high in fat and cholesterol, and can be high in sodium. For vegetarians tofu, beans, lentils, chickpeas, nuts, and other high-protein vegetables make up
this food group.

SO WHAT IS A BALANCED DIET?

When faced with the enormous choice of food that we have today, it seems almost impossible to try to work out what a balanced diet is. Indeed, everyone seems to have their own ideas about what they think is good and what is not. Some people feel that the more food costs, then the better it is for you. This is by no means the case. Others feel that if they manage to fulfill their quota of five portions of fruit and vegetables each day, then they have done enough to eat a good diet. For some, it is eating a cooked meal every day.

Many people, if they are honest, are not really sure what a balanced diet is. Are they eating the right kinds of foods? Is it enough? Sometimes the messages are confusing, but there are a few simple rules:

EAT THREE MEALS A DAY

They need not be the traditional meals, but aim for three separate eating occasions. Space them out so that there are no really long gaps between eating (apart from sleeping). The traditional breakfast, lunch, and evening meal is great if you follow a traditional life pattern. But for many, shifts and odd working hours are the norm, so just rearrange your meals accordingly and, if necessary, use a little ingenuity.

EAT THREE TYPES OF FOOD AT EACH MEAL

Choose something from the protein group (e.g. milk, meat, eggs, cheese, fish, legumes, or nuts), then select something from the fruit and vegetable group, and finally, but very importantly, something from the carbohydrate group, such as potatoes, cereals, breads, rice, and pasta.

EAT A VARIETY OF FOOD

The greater the variety of foods, the better the chance of getting a wide variety of vitamins. With fruit and vegetables, the more different colors they are, the better they are for you nutritionally.

AND FINALLY ...

Think SAS as your dietary watchword. These products are OK to consume in sensible amounts:

Spreading fats

Low-fat spreads, butter, and cooking oils for example. Use in small amounts because they are great for providing fat-soluble vitamins and essential fatty acid.

Alcohol

Drink modestly and wisely.

Sugar and sugar-containing foods

The odd treat now and then is acceptable, especially if you need to keep your calories up, if you are prone to be underweight, or if you exercise a lot.

Take a look at the recipe ideas later in the book for some simple ideas showing how it all fits together.

NUTRIENTS AT RISK

There are some nutrients that are vital for health and which need special mention. They are:

Iron

Iron-deficiency anemia is a relatively common deficiency. It is most commonly found in teenage girls and women. High menstrual blood loss and a poor diet cause anemia, especially if iron-rich foods are not often eaten. Typical symptoms are fatigue, and the person can be paler in skin color, although this symptom is not always easy to spot.

Iron-deficiency anemia is far more common than it used to be because there has been a shift away from eating red meat to choosing chicken or even vegetarian options. Vegetable-based diets need not be low in iron if carefully balanced. There is an increasing trend toward snacking during the day and eating fewer meals, so though not every choice has to be perfect, eating too many foods that are not ideal is unwise.

Avoid becoming anemic by eating some lean red meat each week. If you favor a vegetarian diet, choose eggs, which are rich in iron, for one or two meals a week. Legumes, e.g. beans of all kinds, peas, and lentils, are very good sources of iron. Always include plenty of fruit and vegetables with your meals because they increase the amount of iron that the body absorbs from food. Breakfast cereals are usually fortified with iron equivalent to 25–33 percent of the daily requirement for adult females. You need not have them at breakfast; eat them as a snack during the day or at bedtime.

Calcium

Bones constantly repair themselves throughout life. Bone growth is greatest during childhood, and relative to their size children's need for calcium is high. There is a constant cycle of bone growth, repair, and bone loss, but bone density tends to decline after the age of thirty-five. Therefore dietary calcium intake is more important after that age to maintain good bone strength. There is considerable debate over the amount of calcium that is required by adults. Research suggests that the official recommended daily allowance is set too low, and we should be consuming more than 1,000 mg daily.

Osteoporosis results from a person having a low bone-mineral content, causing bones to fracture easily. It is commonly found in women after their menopause, as the hormones responsible for regular menstruation also play a role in maintaining bone strength. Men are not immune from osteoporosis, but because they have bigger skeletons than women, it takes a little longer for them to reach the critical level at which osteoporosis becomes a problem.

Osteoporosis can become a problem in people who don't get enough calcium. There are many individuals

who choose to drop milk from their diet, commonly because they want to lose weight. However, there are also people who may be allergic or intolerant to milk and are not taking corrective steps to ensure they are getting enough calcium. Because milk is such a valuable source of calcium, it is unwise to omit it from the diet without good reason. Lower-fat varieties of milk are just as good sources of calcium as whole milk, and if allergy or an intolerance appears to be a problem, then get your diet checked out by a professionally qualified dietitian. They can suggest ways of increasing the levels if they are low.

Finally, we know that exercise is good because it strengthens bones. However, avoid smoking and excessive alcohol because these weaken the bones.

Folic Acid/Folate

Deficiency of folic acid or folate is not a recognized medical condition. However, it is considered prudent for women who are planning to have a baby to take folic acid supplements as this will help reduce the risk of neural tube defects, such as spina bifida. It is also thought that diets high in folic acid may help to reduce the risk of heart disease. One of the richest sources of this vitamin is fruit and vegetables. We also know that fruit and vegetables may have other heart-protective factors.

DO I NEED VITAMIN AND MINERAL SUPPLEMENTS?

The simple answer is no, as long as you are following the guidelines on foods set out in this book. However, if you feel that you would like a little reassurance, then choose a multivitamin and mineral preparation. There are many available at the drugstore and in supermarkets and either taking one every other day or even taking half a tablet each day is sufficient. Before taking any supplements check with your doctor.

FUNCTIONAL FOODS

These are defined as foods that have health-giving properties over and above their nutritional value. Those presently available are the new margarines enriched with "stanols" or "sterols" that could help to lower cholesterol levels, and, for women, breads with phytoestrogens added by enriching the bread with soy and linseed. This bread has been recommended for women who want to avoid using synthetic hormones to help to reduce some of the problems associated with the menopause.

Other interesting foods in this group are the new range of fermented milks and yogurts with live (probiotic) bacteria that can survive in the digestive system. These foods have been used to grow beneficial bacteria in the intestines and are specifically useful in individuals who have had food poisoning or have been taking antibiotics.

ENERGY & BODY WEIGHT

Are you the right weight for your height? There are charts available for you to check or you can work out your body mass index (BMI).

To do this, divide your weight (in pounds) by your height (in inches squared) and multiply the figure by 703. Alternatively, divide your weight (in kg) by your height (in meters squared):

HOW YOU SHAPE UP

BMI (BODY MASS INDEX) =

$$\frac{\text{weight in pounds}}{\text{(height in inches)} \times \text{(height in inches)}} \times 703$$

OR

$$\frac{\text{weight in kilograms}}{\text{(height in meters)} \times \text{(height in meters)}}$$

For example, a person who weighs 140 lb and is 67 in tall has a BMI of 22.5

$$\frac{140\ \text{lb}}{\text{(67 in)} \times \text{(67 in)}} \times 703$$

Below 18.5	underweight (may harm your health)
18.5–24.9	normal weight range (within the healthy range)
25.0–29.9	overweight (losing weight is recommended)
Over 30	obese (may harm your health)

(Calculation of BMI source: Centers for Disease Control and Prevention, 2008)

WAIST CIRCUMFERENCE

MEN
Waist circumference over 37 in (94 cm) indicates a **slight** health risk

Waist circumference over 40 in (102 cm) indicates a **substantial** health risk

WOMEN
Waist circumference over 31½ in (80 cm) indicates a **slight** health risk

Waist circumference over 34½ in (88 cm) indicates a **substantial** health risk

KNOW HOW MANY CALORIES YOU SHOULD EAT

To avoid gaining weight over time, you should aim to burn up as many calories through basic metabolic function and physical activity as you take in. To know whether you're on track, you need to be able to estimate how many calories you need based on your age, gender, and level of physical activity.

The calorie ranges shown in this table allow for the needs of people of different ages within an age group. Adults need fewer calories at older ages. For example, an active 31-year-old man needs about 3,000 daily calories, but an active 50-year-old man needs only about 2,800 calories.

ACTIVITY LEVEL AND ESTIMATED CALORIES BURNED				
Gender	Age (years)	Sedentary[1]	Moderately Active[2]	Active[3]
Female	19–30	2,000	2,000–2,200	2,400
	31–50	1,800	2,000	2,200
	51+	1,600	1,800	2,000–2,200
Male	19–30	2,400	2,600–2,800	3,000
	31 50	2,200	2,400–2,600	2,800–3,000
	51+	2,200	2,200–2,400	2,400–2,800

1 Sedentary means you have a lifestyle that includes only the light physical activity associated with typical day-to-day life.
2 Moderately active means you have a lifestyle that includes physical activity equivalent to walking about 1.5 to 3 miles per day at 3 to 4 miles per hour, in addition to the light physical activity associated with typical day-to-day life.
3 Active means you have a lifestyle that includes physical activity equivalent to walking more than 3 miles per day at 3 to 4 miles per hour, in addition to the light physical activity associated with typical day-to-day life.

To lose weight, subtract about 500 calories from your daily requirement and use the calorie counter to check your intake. Very low-calorie diets (below 1,200) are not a good way to lose weight. By making a smaller adjustment, you will lose weight more slowly but have a better chance of long-term success.

Note: These guidelines are only for adults—children need a proportionately higher calorie intake. Before starting any diet, check with your physician.

LOSING WEIGHT SAFELY

If you're trying to lose weight, you're not alone. Over 61 percent of adults in the United States were classified as overweight (BMI over 25) or obese (BMI over 30). The number of obese people in the country has doubled in the last two decades.

Many nutritionists believe that the reason for this alarming rise is due not to our eating more, but to our doing less. Modern technology and labor-saving devices mean that we're much less active than we used to be. Our weight is a reflection of the balance between the energy (calories) we consume and the energy we use. Our energy intake is determined by the amount and type of food we eat. Our energy expenditure is determined by a combination of our resting metabolic rate and the amount of calories we burn in day-to-day activities.

The resting metabolic rate is the amount of energy our body needs during rest or sleep. This is similar to the fuel used by a car when the engine is idling but the car is stationary. If our energy intake equals our energy expenditure, our body weight will remain the same, but if our intake exceeds our expenditure, the excess energy is stored in the body as fat (see page 22).

THE SEESAW EFFECT

Weight gain
If energy intake is greater than energy expenditure, the seesaw will tip at an angle, i.e. weight gain.

Weight loss
If energy expenditure is greater than energy intake, the seesaw will tip in the opposite direction, i.e. weight loss.

Weight maintenance
If energy expenditure equals energy intake, the seesaw will be flat, i.e. weight maintenance.

energy intake, i.e. calories consumed

energy expenditure, i.e. a combination of metabolic rate and physical activities

THE IDEAL RATE OF WEIGHT LOSS

Experts agree the best and safest way to lose weight is slowly and steadily between 1–2 lb (0.5–1 kg) a week is the ideal rate. If you lose too much weight too quickly, there is a danger of losing lean muscle tissue as well as fat. Since our basal metabolic rate (the number of calories the body needs to function) is related to the amount of lean muscle tissue we have, it's a good idea to do whatever we can to preserve it.

HOW LOW SHOULD YOU GO?

The total number of calories we need to eat each day varies, depending on a number of factors, including age, weight, sex, activity levels, body composition, and metabolic rate. As a general guide, women need around 2,400 calories a day and men need 3,000. To lose 1 lb (0.5 kg) a week, you need to reduce your calorie intake by 500 calories a day. Diets that restrict calories too severely (fewer than 1,200 calories a day) are not recommended.

HOW YOU SHAPE UP

Although most of us can get a pretty good idea of whether we need to lose weight or not just by looking in the mirror, you can get a more accurate assessment by calculating your Body Mass Index or measuring your waist circumference (see panel on page 18).

THE THREE MAIN REASONS THAT DIETS FAIL

Setting unrealistic goals

If you set unrealistic goals, you're more likely to become disheartened and give up. Aim for a slow but steady weight loss of 1–2 lb (0.5–1 kg) a week. If you lose too much weight too quickly, there's a danger of losing lean muscle tissue as well as fat.

Following the wrong kind of diet

However tempting they may seem, crash diets just don't work. Although you may lose weight initially, you'll find that you will end up putting on not just the weight you originally lost but even more.

Not eating enough

A mistake people often make is to reduce their calorie intake too severely. Overly strict diets are difficult to stick to in the long run, they're not necessary, and they're not healthy. If you restrict your calories too severely, the chances are that you'll end up missing important nutrients.

UNDERSTANDING YOUR RELATIONSHIP WITH FOOD

Often we eat out of habit or to satisfy emotional needs rather than because we are hungry. We use food to celebrate, to relieve boredom, or to make us feel better when we're unhappy or lonely. Certain people, places, moods, and situations can also prompt us to eat.

Keeping a food diary will help you to identify these external cues. Buy a notebook and divide the pages into columns. Keep a record of everything you eat and drink and how you feel for two weeks.

FOOD DIARY		
Date	Monday	Tuesday
Time	3.30pm	10.30am
Where were you?	At home	At work
What were you doing?	Nothing	Trying to meet a deadline
Who were you with?	No one	Work colleagues
How did you feel?	Bored	Stressed
What did you eat?	Potato chips	Chocolate bar
How hungry were you? (On a scale of 1–5)	5	4

1 = hungry, 5 = not hungry

At the end of two weeks, review your diary and make a list of all the triggers that prompt you to eat when you're not really hungry.

Once you have identified these trigger factors, you can start to think about solutions and ways to avoid those situations in future. Work out strategies that will help avoid or change the way you behave when faced with these triggers. If, for instance, you find you get home after work so hungry that you end up eating a family-size package of cheesy snacks while preparing the evening meal, plan ahead. Have a healthy snack, such as a banana or yogurt, before you leave the office so you won't feel so hungry when you get home.

If your diary reveals that you use food as a way of making yourself feel better when you're unhappy or depressed, make a list of nonfood-related activities that will help to lift your spirits when you're feeling low. Rent a movie, have a manicure, or take a long leisurely bath rather than reaching for a chocolate bar.

KEEPING THE FAT DOWN

Choose lower-fat milks. Milk is good for you and your bones so don't give it up, just choose reduced-fat or skim milks.

Use a lower-fat spread on breads

Don't give up spreads altogether because they provide useful fat-soluble vitamins.

Keep fried foods to the minimum

Cooking in oil, even if it is polyunsaturated, still adds calories. Broil or bake in the oven instead.

Trim visible fat from meats and avoid large helpings

Meat is not bad for you if eaten wisely. It provides useful vitamins and minerals.

Cut out baked goods

Cakes, cookies, and pies are usually high in fat.

Avoid mayonnaise

Often used in sandwiches or on salads, it is high in fat and can easily be avoided.

If you are a cheese lover, ration it

Just eat a small piece for each meal, and grate it so it looks more. Some lower-fat cheeses can make good substitutes, but sometimes at the expense of flavor.

KEEPING THE CALORIES DOWN
Use artificial sweeteners instead of sugar—you can save as much as 20 calories per teaspoon.

Choose diet soft drinks
Avoid the ordinary variety. Check out the differences and you will be amazed at how many calories you can save.

Avoid desserts
Choose fresh fruit or a yogurt, which have much fewer calories (a really tempting dessert can easily set you back 500 calories). Desserts read "stressed" backward!

Try to avoid snacks between meals
The extra calories soon add up. If you enjoy snacks, then make sure you don't overindulge at mealtimes.

Keep an eye on your "portion control"
Does your plate look really full, or are you going back for seconds?

Don't miss meals
Skip a meal and you are more likely to snack or overeat on the next occasion.

MAKING DIETS WORK FOR YOU

Tackling dieting on your own can be tough. If you can, seek help from a sympathetic and good friend. You must also help yourself by not becoming a diet bore. Diet bores are their own worst enemy. They think and talk about their diet all the time, a good way to lose friends and support! Try being diplomatic—you may not mention you are on a diet to your friends. Some may not notice, especially if you are not making too many changes to your usual eating pattern.

If you are trying to lose weight, it can sometimes take a little while for people to notice a weight change and by that time you can be well on your way to losing "real" weight. If you are simply trying to improve your eating habits, then gradual changes are the best and are far more successful in the long term. Remember, Rome was not built in a day.

THINGS TO DO

If you feel like eating something, then maybe you should have a list of handy distractions. The list can be anything from reading a book, tidying out that drawer, getting out an address book and phoning a friend, or enjoying some aromatherapy treatment. These may just help you from straying from your good intentions.

MOTIVATIONAL TIPS

Try making a list of motivational tips to help you with your diet. Here are some ideas to begin with.

Choose wisely

One bad meal choice or mistake doesn't make a bad diet. Likewise, watch out for the "all or nothing situation." If you have eaten a piece of chocolate, you don't have to eat the rest of the bar or box.

Take your time

It takes 15–20 minutes for the body to register satisfaction, so wait before you decide whether you are really hungry and need a second helping or not.

Don't become afraid of food

Food is to be enjoyed, so learn to enjoy and take pleasure from foods that you know are better for your health.

Enjoy your diet

If there is a food on your diet, that you are supposed to eat but you don't like it, find a good substitute. If you don't enjoy your diet, you won't keep to it.

Never make your target for weight-loss unrealistic

Aim for a small loss, achieve that, and then go on to lose more if you want to. Remember, you did not get fat overnight so you won't lose weight overnight, either.

Be proud of small achievements

If weight loss was easy nobody would be fat, so if you have achieved a loss, no matter how small, you are quite remarkable and should be proud of your efforts.

Feel good about yourself

You have made a conscious effort to make a change, so pat yourself on the back. Take one day at a time and congratulate yourself for what you have achieved on that day.

No excuses

Don't use your "heavy" bones or build as a reason for being big; it is only you that you are kidding.

Shopping list

When shopping, use a list and keep to those foods you know you need. Don't buy something you know you will regret. Avoid shopping when you're hungry—you may buy more than you really need.

Be shop-wise

Don't be tempted by special offers on foods you don't need— the supermarkets are interested in profits, not your waistline.

FOOD LABELING

To find out what is in a food before we buy, we look at the label. But almost without exception people find food labels very confusing. Food labels are supposed to provide information to allow you to make a sensible choice, and to compare different foods.

HOW TO READ FOOD LABELS

So what do you need to look for? The label should describe the food and not misrepresent its contents, e.g. if it is described as "meat and potato," then there should be more meat than potato. You will be able to see this by looking at the ingredients.

The contents list

Contents should be listed in quantity order. Therefore, the food in the largest amount should be listed first, with the smallest quantity of an ingredient listed last. If a food states "no added sugar," then that is what it means. However, labeling is not so straightforward, such as on "no added sugar" yogurts.

A quick glance down the nutrition information list shows that sugar is in fact contained and panic thus sets in. Sugar content needs to be checked more closely because with milk and fruit make it complicated.

When foods are analyzed for sugars, the total sugar content includes milk sugars (lactose) and fruit sugars (fructose) as well as the familiar sugar (sucrose). Typically, an individual container of yogurt with sugar added will have approximately 20 g of sugar per serving (10 g of that is added sugar); if no sugar is added, then the sugar content will be 10 g, this 10 g coming from milk and fruit sugars. Milk and fruit sugars are used in the body in a slightly different way from ordinary sugar and should not be of concern to people with diabetes.

Where to start

We read the nutrition label first. There is plenty of nutrition information but we are really only interested in calories and fat, which is why some manufacturers include a special panel for only calories and fat. The separate panel also states the typical calories and fat that adult females and males should consume.

Nutritional information is given per 100 g and/or per suggested portion size so you can work out how much you are eating. You can work out how much fat you are eating as a percentage of the food's total calories. It is very simple and all you need to know is the amount of calories and fat in any food and the calorie value of fat: 1 g of fat provides 9 calories (1 g of protein provides 4 calories, and 1 g of carbohydrate provides 4 calories). The rest is simple mathematics …

The information

For carbohydrates, the first figure given is the total amount of carbohydrate in the product. Giving information on sugars helps in choosing items with a lower sugar content.

Fats are presented as total fat, trans fats, and saturated fats in the products, and may also state how much is saturated. Information on saturates is helpful, because any fat that is not saturated will be mono- or polyunsaturated.

NUTRITIONAL FACTS PANEL

Serving size (as cups, g)
Servings per container
    (per person)
Calories (value)
Total fat (g and %)
    Trans fats (g and %)
    Saturated fats (g and %)
Cholesterol (mg and %)
Sodium (g and %)
Total carbohydrates (g and %)
    Dietary fiber (g and %)
    Sugar (g and %)
Protein (g and %)
Vitamin A (%)
Vitamin C (%)
Calcium (%)
Iron (%)

Percentage (%) of daily value, based on a 2,000-calorie diet.

USING THE COUNTER

The A–Z food counter in this book lists the carbohydrate, fiber, and fat content in grams per weight/average serving of food. If the food has no typical serving, a 100 g amount is given. Everyone's fat and carbohydrate requirements differ slightly depending on their individual daily energy (calorie) needs. To calculate your own daily calorie count see page 19.

EAT FEWER SATURATED AND TRANS FATS
Although a small amount of fat is needed in our diet to provide essential vitamins and fatty acids that our bodies cannot alone provide, most people need to reduce the saturated fat they eat. It is important to understand about the different fats we eat, so that we can make healthier food choices.

There are two types of fat in the diet: the unsaturated fats include polyunsaturated and monounsaturated fats and the saturated fats are the fats we should be eating less of because they raise blood cholesterol levels which can cause the blood to thicken and clot. Narrowing arteries and clots (also called thrombus) can result in a heart attack or stroke.

Saturated fats are found mainly in dairy products such as butter, cheese, yogurt, cream, milk, and meat but also in a few vegetable oils such as coconut and

palm oil, hard margarines, and lard, and are "hidden" in processed foods like cookies and chocolate.

Unsaturated fats can be either polyunsaturated or monounsaturated, and both play an important role in a healthy diet to replace saturated oils. There are two types of polyunsaturated fats. The first is found in the seeds of plants such as the sunflowerseed and soy oil and is called omega-6. The second type comes mainly from oily fish and is called omega-3.

Monounsaturated fats have been found to lower the amount of bad cholesterol in the blood. Monounsaturated fats can be found mainly in olive oil, avocados, and nuts.

THE TRANS-FATTY ACIDS ISSUE

Recently, there has been concern that the process called hydrogenation, in which various vegetable and animal oils are turned into solids to make margarine or spreads, leads to the formation of trans-fatty acids. These are treated in the body in the same way as saturated fats and so may raise the level of cholesterol if eaten in large quantities. Currently, we are advised to use a fat low in saturated fat and containing higher levels of polyunsaturated or monounsaturated fats. If possible, look carefully at the nutritional labeling

and choose a product whose trans-fatty acids and saturated fat levels are less than 15 percent.

COUNTING FAT
A woman who needs 2,400 calories a day will require about 720 calories (30 percent) to come from fats. If 1 gram fat = 9 calories, the desired fat intake would be 80 g/day. A man using a base figure of 3,000 calories needs no more than 100 g fat.

CARBOHYDRATE
Carbohydrate is the body's instant-energy fuel. That which is not immediately required is stored as fat. The digestion of carbohydrates provides glucose, which is the preferred fuel of the body.

Carbohydrates comprise starchy and sugary foods. Staple foods worldwide, such as bread, rice, potatoes, millet, pasta, cassava, yam, plantains, and green bananas, are starchy carbohydrates. High-protein beans, lentils, seeds, and nuts also contain starchy carbohydrates.

Natural sugars are present in milk and many plant foods, especially fruit. Concentrated or pure sugars, occurring in honey and cane/beet sugars are high in calories, but of little nutritional value.

Note: Although sugar provides a quicker supply of glucose than starchy foods, excess sugar (extrinsic sugars) can lead to dental decay and obesity.

COUNTING CARBOHYDRATES

A recommended 45–65 percent of daily energy should come from carbohydrates (with the least from pure sugars).

FIBER

Vital for the bowel to function normally, fiber is also known to help lower blood fats (lipids), helping to reduce the risk of heart disease. This is the fibrous part of plant foods (cereals, fruit, vegetables, legumes, nuts, seeds) that remains in the intestine after digestion. Fiber helps to prevent constipation, coronary heart disease, gallbladder disease, and some cancers.

The recommended intake of dietary fiber is an average of 25–30 g/day. To achieve this, eat plenty of bread, cereals, and potatoes, as well as five portions of fruit and vegetables.

Note: Too much fiber can reduce the absorption of some minerals. It is also important to drink plenty of fluids. Aim for a minimum of 8 cups/approx. 2 liters per day.

VITAMINS & MINERALS

Some vitamins are soluble in fat and hence known as fat-soluble vitamins (and are only found in fat-containing foods), while others are water-soluble. Excess fat-soluble vitamins are normally stored in the liver, while excess water-soluble vitamins are excreted. It is difficult to have an overdose of water-soluble vitamins, but "mega" dosing on vitamins is not generally regarded to be wise. There is very little scientific data to prove that it has any health benefits. Vitamins and minerals work together. It can be harmful to take large doses of one nutrient because it may affect the action of another.

Some vitamins are known as antioxidants. These have a very important role in the body by helping to protect against molecular damage caused by "free radicals." Free radicals, which are harmful, can accumulate in the body as the result of exposure to car exhaust fumes, the sun's ultraviolet rays, cigarette smoke, and excess alcohol.

ESSENTIAL VITAMINS & MINERALS

These are the main vitamins and minerals you need. A good varied diet should contain these and other vitamins and minerals required in much smaller amounts.

VITAMIN A (Retinol)

FUNCTION	Helps vision in dim light and to maintain healthy skin and surface tissues. In excess it can be poisonous. Supplements should not be taken in pregnancy.
TO BE FOUND IN	Liver, fish oils, dairy produce, and egg yolks.

VITAMIN B1 THIAMINE

FUNCTION	All B vitamins are essential for enzyme systems and metabolism.
TO BE FOUND IN	Animal and vegetable foods, such as milk, organ meats, pork, eggs, vegetables, fruit, whole-grain cereals, and fortified breakfast cereals.

VITAMIN B2 RIBOFLAVIN

FUNCTION	All B vitamins are essential for enzyme systems and metabolism.
TO BE FOUND IN	In foods, especially of animal origin. Milk is a particularly important source for many people.

VITAMIN B3 NIACIN

FUNCTION	All B vitamins are essential for enzyme systems and metabolism.
TO BE FOUND IN	Widely distributed. Found in cereals, meat, fish, dairy products.

VITAMIN C (Ascorbic acid)

FUNCTION	Essential for healthy connective tissue. Deficiency results in bleeding gums etc.
TO BE FOUND IN	Vegetables and fruit, especially citrus fruit, guavas, and black currants.

VITAMIN D (Cholecalciferol)

FUNCTION	Needed for the absorption of calcium into the blood and maintenance of bones. In children deficiency of vitamin D leads to rickets, and in adults to osteomalacia.
TO BE FOUND IN	Main source is the action of sunlight on the skin and most people require no more than this. Natural dietary sources are all of animal origin, such as fish and animal livers and oils, fatty fish, butter, milk, and eggs. It may be added to some foods as a supplement.

FOLIC ACID

FUNCTION	Essential for cell growth, especially in pregnancy. Deficiency may lead to a form of anemia.
TO BE FOUND IN	Organ meats, yeast extract, green leafy vegetables

CALCIUM

FUNCTION	Essential for the maintenance of bones and connective tissue. Deficiency may accelerate osteoporosis.
TO BE FOUND IN	Milk, cheese, and yogurt are best sources. Also occurs in fruit, vegetables, and seeds. May be added to bread and flour.

IRON

FUNCTION	Essential for the prevention of anemia.
TO BE FOUND IN	Present in a wide range of foods, especially proteins—meat and dairy foods.

ZINC

FUNCTION	Helps wound healing and enzyme activity.
TO BE FOUND IN	Present in a wide range of foods, especially proteins—meat and dairy foods.

VITAMINS IN DETAIL

VITAMIN A
(retinol: fat-soluble; carotenes: water-soluble)
Average requirement: Women and men 600 mcg per day (more if pregnant or breast-feeding).

Vitamin A is important for cell growth and development, and for the formation of visual pigments in the eye. Carotenes are an important antioxidant. There are several, of which beta-carotene is the best known. Good sources: Retinol is found in liver, meat and meat products, whole milk and its products, e.g. cheese and butter, and eggs. Beta-carotene is found in red and yellow fruit and vegetables, e.g. carrots, bell peppers, mangoes, and apricots.

Note: Women who are pregnant should avoid Vitamin A supplements and liver or liver products, because it is known that excess intakes of the vitamin may cause birth defects. If taking a supplement, ensure that it is no more than 100 percent RDA.

VITAMIN B1
(thiamine: water-soluble)
Average requirement: Women and men 1 mg per day.

Important to enable the release of energy from carbohydrate-containing foods. Good sources include yeast and yeast products, bread, fortified breakfast cereals, and potatoes.

Note: The amount of thiamine required is directly linked to the amount of carbohydrate eaten in the diet. Thiamine deficiency is very unlikely except where alcohol is a major part of the diet.

VITAMIN B2
(riboflavin: water-soluble)
Average requirement: Women and men 1.3 mg per day (more if pregnant or breast-feeding).

Important for metabolism of carbohydrates, proteins, and fats to produce energy. Good sources are meat, yeast extracts, fortified breakfast cereals, milk, milk products.

Note: Riboflavin in milk is easily destroyed by exposure to sunlight, so keep milk out of the sunlight!

VITAMIN B3
(niacin: water-soluble)
Average requirement: Women and men 18 mg per day.

Required for the metabolism of food into energy. Good sources are milk and milk products, fortified breakfast cereals, legumes, meat, poultry, and eggs.

Note: It is uncommon to have a dietary deficiency of this vitamin.

VITAMIN B5
(pantothenic acid: water-soluble)
Average requirement: Women and men 3–7 mg per day.

Important for metabolism of food into energy. Good sources: Most foods, especially fortified breakfast cereals, whole-grain bread, and dairy products.

Note: There has been no evidence of deficiency of this vitamin because it is found in so many foods.

VITAMIN B6
(pyridoxine: water-soluble)
Average requirement: Women and men 1.5 mg per day.

Important for metabolism of protein and fat. It may also be involved with the regulation of sex hormones. Good sources are liver, fish, pork, soybeans, and peanuts.

Note: Drugs containing penicillin or estrogen may increase the need for B6. It is also thought to help some women who have PMS. Regular high doses have been known to cause some peripheral nerve damage.

VITAMIN B12
(cyanocobalamin: water-soluble)
Average requirement: Women and men 1.5 mcg per day (more if pregnant or breast-feeding).

Important for production of red blood cells and DNA and vital for growth and the nervous system. Good sources are meat, fish, eggs, poultry, and milk. There are no plant sources of this vitamin.

Note: Supplements are recommended for vegans. The metabolic functions are closely associated with those of folic acid.

FOLIC ACID
(B vitamin: water-soluble)
Average requirement: Women and men 200 mcg per day (more if pregnant or breast-feeding).

Folic acid is important for protein metabolism, and in the development of the neural tube in the fetus during the early stages of pregnancy. Good sources are whole-grain cereals, fortified breakfast cereals, green leafy vegetables, oranges, and liver.

Note: It is recommended to take a daily supplement of 400 mcg of folic acid prior to conception and during the first 13 weeks of pregnancy. It is also thought that folic acid may play a role in helping to prevent heart disease.

BIOTIN
(B group: water-soluble)
Average requirement: Women and men 0.15 mg per day.

Important for the metabolism of fatty acids. Good sources are liver, kidney, eggs, and nuts. Microorganisms also manufacture this vitamin in the digestive system.

Note: A protein found in raw egg binds with the biotin to make it unavailable and prevents the body from utilizing it.

VITAMIN C
(ascorbic acid: water-soluble)
Average requirement: Women and men 60 mg per day.

Important for healing wounds and the formation of collagen and is a major component of skin, muscle, and bone. Also an important antioxidant. Good sources are citrus fruit, "soft summer" fruit, vegetables, and potatoes.

Note: It is thought that high doses (1,000 mg/1 g) help reduce the severity of the common cold. However, at those levels it may irritate the stomach lining, causing diarrhea or renal stones.

VITAMIN D
(cholecalciferol and ergocalciferol: fat-soluble)
Average requirement: Women and men 5 mcg per day.

Important for absorption and handling of calcium to help build bone strength. Good sources are oily fish, eggs, whole milk and milk products, margarine. The manufacture of vitamin D just under the skin is very important.

Note: Elderly, housebound people and those who are covered up even in sunny weather may need supplements to obtain the recommended amounts.

VITAMIN E
(tocopherol: fat-soluble)
Average requirement: Women and men 10 mg per day.

Important as an antioxidant, helping to protect cell membranes from damage. Good sources are vegetable oils, margarine, seeds, nuts, and green vegetables.

Note: High doses of this vitamin have not been shown to cause any health problems, even though it is a fat-soluble vitamin.

MINERALS IN DETAIL

Like vitamins, minerals are required in small amounts but are essential to good health.

CALCIUM

Average requirement: Women and men 800 mg per day (more if breast-feeding).

Important for healthy bones and teeth, nerve transmission, muscle contraction, blood clotting, and hormone function. Good sources are dairy products, small fish bones, nuts, legumes, fortified white flours and bread, green leafy vegetables.

   Note: People who have low calcium intakes and do little exercise are at risk of osteoporosis later in life. This applies especially to women who have passed the menopause. Abnormal deposits of calcium can occur if the diet is very high in vitamin D.

IRON

Average requirement: Women 14.8 mg per day.
Men 8.7 mg per day.

Iron is a key building block of hemoglobin, which carries oxygen around the body and is therefore vital for normal growth and development. Good sources are liver, corned beef, red meat, fortified breakfast cereals, legumes, green leafy vegetables, egg yolk, cocoa, and cocoa products.

Note: Eating foods rich in vitamin C helps improve iron absorption from vegetable-based foods.

MAGNESIUM

Average requirement: Women and men 300 mg per day.

Important for the efficient functioning of metabolic enzymes, development of the skeleton, and nerve/muscle transmission. Good sources are nuts, green vegetables, meat, cereals, milk, and yogurt.

Note: Women with PMS (premenstrual syndrome) may benefit from extra magnesium.

ZINC

Average requirement: Women and men 15 mg per day.

Important for metabolism and for healing wounds. A deficiency is thought to be related to male infertility, because quite high levels are found in the prostate gland. Good sources are liver, meat, legumes, whole-grain cereals, nuts, and oysters.

Note: Low zinc intakes may result in a poor sense of taste; prolonged high doses may cause copper deficiency.

IODINE
Average requirement: Women and men 140 mcg per day.

Important for the manufacture of thyroid hormones and for normal development. Good sources are seafood, seaweed, milk, and dairy products.

Note: The absorption of iodine may be reduced by foods that contain goitrogens. These are found in foods such as peaches, almonds, soybeans, and cassava. Dietary deficiencies are rare in the United States.

SELENIUM
Average requirement: Women and men 75 mcg per day.

Important antioxidant mineral that forms part of an enzyme system found in red blood cells. Good sources are liver, kidney, meat, eggs, cereals, nuts, and dairy products.

Note: Supplements with more than 100 mcg should be avoided because they can cause toxicity.

POTASSIUM
Average requirement: Women and men 3,500mg per day

Important for the normal transmission of nerve-muscle signals. Good sources are fruit, vegetables, milk, and bread.

Note: Diets high in potassium may protect against high blood pressure.

SODIUM

Average requirement: Women and men 1,600 mg per day.

Important in helping to control body fluid and balance, and involved in muscle and nerve function. All food are sources, but processed, pickled, and salted foods are the richest sources.

Note: Many people consume more salt than is required, so it is best to avoid foods known to be salty. Adding salt to food at the table is not advisable.

TRACE ELEMENTS

These are a group of nutrients that are essential to health but only required in very small amounts. It is quite difficult to establish how much the body needs and indeed if the body needs them every day. It is most likely that a healthy diet will provide all the trace elements that a typical body needs.

PHYTONUTRIENTS

In recent years, there has been a considerable amount of interest and research into a group of nutrients often known as phytonutrients—"phyto" means "plant." It is thought that there are a number of exciting new chemicals that are found only in plants that may be beneficial to health. An example is the recent research into a substance called lycopene, which is found in tomatoes. This nutrient may have a role in helping to prevent prostate cancer. Similarly, estrogens found in some foods, especially soy, may help to prevent some of the symptoms of the menopause. Much of this research is still in the early stages; suffice to say that it suggests we should be eating more fruit and vegetables.

OMEGA OILS

There is increasing evidence that a diet including omega oils is good for health, benefiting people with heart disease and arthritis. They are found in oily fish, such as herring, mackerel, salmon, sardines, pilchards, and trout. Fish such as cod, flounder, haddock, and even tuna have relatively low levels of omega oils. For those people who do not like oily fish, a fish oil supplement may be preferable. If you eat oily fish only once a week, then take a supplement every other day.

RAW VERSUS COOKED VEGETABLES

Cooking is known to destroy water-soluble vitamins, but by eating raw vegetables are you getting more vitamins? The simple answer is no. Scientific studies have shown that cooking helps break down the cell walls to allow vitamins and minerals to be absorbed more easily by the digestive system. We would have to do a lot of chewing to break down the cell walls so easily. But keep cooking to a minimum to maximize the uptake of vitamins.

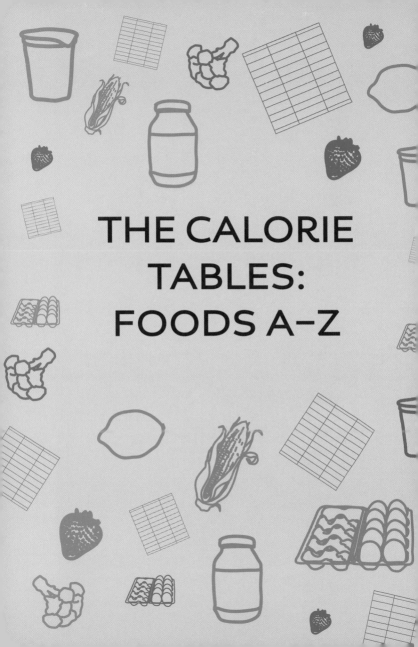

THE CALORIE
TABLES:
FOODS A–Z

FOOD	FAT g	FIBER g	CARB g	ENERGY kcal

ALCOHOL

BEER

lager, 12 fl oz	0	1	6	107
light beer, 12 fl oz	0	0	5	99
malt, 12 fl oz	0	0	12	167
pale ale, 12 fl oz	0	0	17	179
regular, 12 fl oz	0	1	13	146
stout, 12 fl oz	0	0	13	157

COCKTAILS

bloody mary, 5 fl oz	0	0	5	116
margarita cocktail, 8 fl oz	0	0	32	500
martini, dry, 2 1/2 fl oz	0	0	0	158
screwdriver cocktail, 8 fl oz	0	0	20	194

LIQUEURS

higher strength, (Curaçao, Drambuie) 1 1/2 fl oz	0	0	19	150
lower strength, (cherry brandy, coffee) 1 1/2 fl oz	0	0	14	108

LIQUORS

bourbon 80 proof, 1 1/2 fl oz	0	0	0	96

FOOD	FAT g	FIBER g	CARB g	ENERGY kcal
gin 80 proof, 1 1/2 fl oz	0	0	0	96
rum 80 proof, 1 1/2 fl oz	0	0	0	96
tequila, 80 proof, 1 1/2 fl oz	0	0	0	96
vodka 80 proof, 1 1/2 fl oz	0	0	0	98
WINES				
champagne, dry, 6 fl oz	0	0	6	126
port, 3 1/2 fl oz	0	0	12	158
red, dry, 6 fl oz	0	0	2	126
rosé, 6 fl oz	0	0	3	122
sherry, dry, 4 fl oz	0	0	4	250
sweet dessert, 4 fl oz	0	0	14	90
vermouth, dry, 1 fl oz	0	0	0	30
vermouth, sweet, 1 fl oz	0	0	4	46
white, medium, 6 fl oz	0	0	1	120
white, sparkling, sweet, 6 fl oz	0	0	12	138
wine cooler, 12 fl oz	0	0	20	170
APPLE				
baked, unsweetened, 1 each	1	5	26	102
dried, 1/4 cup	2	0	14	52
juice, 3/4 cup	0	0	10	68
raw, peeled, 1 each	0.5	2.5	19	73
raw, unpeeled, 1 each	0.5	4	21	81

FOOD	FAT g	FIBER g	CARB g	ENERGY kcal
APRICOT				
canned in juice, 1/2 cup	2	0	15	59
canned in syrup, 4 halves	0	1	15	56
dried, 10 halves	0.5	8	15	66
raw, 3, each	0	2.5	9	37
ARTICHOKE				
globe, boiled, 1 each, 10 1/2 oz	0	6	13	60
Jerusalem, peeled, raw, 1 cup	2	0	26	114
ASPARAGUS				
boiled, 6 spears	0	1	4	22
canned, 1/2 cup	1	2	3	23
AVOCADO				
raw, California, 1 each	30	8	12	306
raw, Florida, 1 each	27	16	27	340

B

BABY FOODS (jars)				
apple & apricots, 4 oz	0	2	15	62
apple & banana, 4 oz	0	2	14	62
apple & raspberry, 4 oz	0	2	18	66
carrot & beef, strained, 4 oz	4	2	4	64

FOOD	FAT g	FIBER g	CARB g	ENERGY kcal
chicken meat, 2½ oz	7	0	0	106
chicken & vegetable dinner, 4 oz	2	2	10	67
fruit dessert, 4 oz	0	1	18	67
mixed vegetables, 4 oz	0	2	8	40
pasta with vegetable dinner, 4 oz	2	2	9	68
rice cereal with apple sauce & banana, 4 oz	0	1	19	90
pork meat—strained 2½ oz	5	0	0	88
BACON				
cooked, 1 oz	14	0	0	163
Canadian (see Pork)				
BAMBOO SHOOTS				
canned, drained, ½ cup	0.5	2	2	13
cooked, ½ cup	0.5	1	2	7
raw, 1 cup	0.5	3.5	8	41
BANANA				
plantain, boiled, ½ cup	0	2	24	89
plantain, raw, 1 each	0	2	24	90
raw, peeled, 1 each	4	0	29	110
BEANS				
adzuki, dried, boiled, ½ cup	0	8	28	147

FOOD	FAT g	FIBER g	CARB g	ENERGY kcal
black-eyed, dried, boiled, 1/2 cup	0	4	16	80
fava, boiled, 1/2 cup	0	5	17	94
green/French, cooked, 1/2 cup	0	2	4	20
green/French, raw, 1 cup	0	4	8	34
lima bean, canned, drained, 1/2 cup	0	7	20	108
navy beans, cooked, 1/2 cup	1	6	24	129
red kidney, canned, 1/2 cup	1	11	24	128
soy, dried, boiled, 1/2 cup	6	5	5	122
BEAN SPROUTS				
alfalfa, raw, 1/2 cup	0.5	1	0	8
mung bean, 1/2 cup	0	1	6	35
BEEF				
chuck roast, trimmed, 3 oz	20	0	0	282
corned, canned, 1 oz	3.5	0	0	61
dried, 1 oz	1	0	0	47
fillet steak, lean, broiled, 3 oz	7	0	0	162
flank, lean, pot-roasted, 3 oz	12	0	0	215
pastrami, 1 oz	0.5	0.5	0	27
rib, prime, roasted, 3 oz	30	0	0	348
rib eye, broiled, 3 oz	19	0	0	261
roast beef, sliced, 1 oz	1	0	0	32

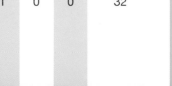

FOOD	FAT g	FIBER g	CARB g	ENERGY kcal
sirloin steak, broiled, 3 oz	11	0	0	185
topside, lean, roast, 3 oz	3	0	0	132
BEET				
boiled, peeled, 1/2 cup	0	2	8	37
pickled, slices, 1/2 cup	0	1	13	53
BELL PEPPERS				
green bell pepper, cooked, 1/2 cup	0	1	5	19
green bell pepper, raw, 1	0.5	3	4	24
red or yellow, raw, 1	0.5	3	10	51
BEVERAGES (HOT)				
cappuccino coffee, 8 fl oz				
- fat-free milk	0	0	7	53
- reduced-fat milk	2	0	7	73
- whole milk	5	0	7	93
chocolate				
- hot chocolate, reduced-fat milk, 6 fl oz	4	0	12	100
- hot chocolate, whole milk, 6 fl oz	7	0	12	134
- instant, low calorie, packet, dry, 1 oz	1	0	4	35

FOOD	FAT g	FIBER g	CARB g	ENERGY kcal
- instant, regular, packet, dry, 1 oz	4	0	18	120
coffee, black, 6 fl oz	0	0	1	4
latte coffee, retail, 8 fl oz				
- whole milk	7	0	11	140
- reduced-fat milk	4	0	11	113
- fat-free milk	0	0	11	80
latte coffee, iced, retail, 6 fl oz				
- fat-free milk	0	0	6	40
- reduced-fat milk	2	0	6	52
- whole milk	3	0	5	64
latte tea, retail, whole milk, 6 fl oz	2	0	21	128
malted milk, powder, 1 oz	1.5	1	21	109
mocha coffee, retail, large, 6 fl oz				
- fat-free milk	4	1	16	116
- reduced-fat milk	6	1	16	136
- whole milk	8	1	16	148
tea, black, 6 fl oz	0	0	0	0
tea, herbal, infusion, 6 fl oz	0	0	0	2

FOOD	FAT g	FIBER g	CARB g	ENERGY kcal
BLACKBERRIES				
canned in heavy syrup, 1/2 cup	0	4	30	118
raw, 1 cup	1	8	18	75
BLACK CURRANTS				
dried, 1/4 cup	0	2	27	102
raw, 1 cup	0	8	17	71
BLUEBERRIES				
raw, 1 cup	1	4	20	81
BOUILLON CUBES				
any, 1 cube	1	0	0.5	12
BRAN (see Cereals)				
BREAD				
bagel, plain, 1, 4 1/2-inch	2	3	59	303
breadsticks, 1, 7 5/8 x 5/8-inch	1	0	7	41
croissant, 1 large	14	2	31	272
focaccia, 1 oz	1.5	1	14	79
French baguette, 1 oz	1	1	14	74
hamburger bun, 1 each	2	1	22	123
muffin, English, 1 each	1	2	26	134
pita, white, 6 1/2-inch diameter	1	1	34	165
pita, wheat, 6 1/2-inch diameter	2	5	35	170
raisin, cinnamon, 1 slice, 1 oz	2.5	2	14	80

FOOD	FAT g	FIBER g	CARB g	ENERGY kcal
rye, 1 slice, 1 oz	1	2	15	83
soda, 1 slice, 1 oz	1	1	16	82
tortilla, corn, (6-inch round) 1	1	1	12	58
tortilla, wheat flour, (6-inch round) 1	0.5	2	20	73
tortilla, white flour, (6-inch round) 1	2	1	18	104
white, 1 slice, 1 oz	1	1	1	67
white dinner roll, 1 oz	2	1	14	84
whole wheat, 1 slice, 1 oz	1	2	13	69
whole wheat roll, 1 each, 1 oz	1	2	15	75
BROCCOLI				
green, boiled, 1/2 cup	0	2	4	22
green, raw, 1 cup	0	2	4	20
BRUSSEL SPROUTS				
boiled, 1/2 cup	1	2	3	27
raw, 1 cup	0.5	4	8	38
BUCKWHEAT KERNELS				
raw, 1/2 cup	3	9	61	292
BULGAR				
(cracked wheat) cooked, 1/2 cup	0.5	4	17	76

FOOD	FAT g	FIBER g	CARB g	ENERGY kcal
BUTTER				
ghee, 1 oz	28.5	0	0	249
salted, 1 tsp	4	0	0	34

C

FOOD	FAT g	FIBER g	CARB g	ENERGY kcal
CABBAGE				
Chinese, raw, shredded, 1 cup	0	1	2	10
green, boiled, 1/2 cup	0	2	2	13
green, raw, 1/2 cup	0	2	3	2
red, boiled, 1/2 cup	0	2	2	11
red, raw, shredded, 1 cup	0	2	3	15
CAKES/PASTRIES/BUNS				
angel food, 1 slice	3	0	29	129
carrot cake, cream cheese topping, 1 piece	27	2	46	437
cheesecake, 1/6 slice	18	0	20	257
chocolate, sponge, without frosting, 1 slice	4	1	36	197
chocolate, with chocolate frosting, 1 slice	11	2	35	235
Danish fruit pastry, 1 each	16	0	45	335

FOOD	FAT g	FIBER g	CARB g	ENERGY kcal
éclair, cream-filled, 1 each,				
5 x 2-inch	16	1	24	262
fruitcake, plain, 1 slice	4	2	27	139
German chocolate, 1 piece	16	2	37	300
gingerbread, 1 piece	12	1	36	263
Greek pastry (baklava), 1 piece,				
2 x 2 x 2½-inch	23	2	29	336
muffin, blueberry, 1 large,				
3¼ x 2¾-inch	5	2	34	197
muffin, chocolate chip, 1 large	9	1	33	230
rice crispie bar, 1 oz	3	0	20	107
yellow, with vanilla frosting,				
⅛ piece	9	0	38	239
CARROTS				
boiled, ½ cup	0	2	3	19
canned, ½ cup	0	1	4	18
raw baby, 2 oz	0	1	4	24
raw, 1 med.	0	2	4	22
CAULIFLOWER				
boiled, ½ cup	0	1	1	17
raw, 1 cup	0	2	4	34

FOOD	FAT g	FIBER g	CARB g	ENERGY kcal
CELERIAC				
boiled, 1/2 cup	0	1	8	32
raw, 1 cup	0	3	14	60
CELERY				
boiled, 1/2 cup	0	2	0.5	6
raw, 1 stalk	0	0.5	0.5	2
CEREALS/BARS				
blueberry, fat-free, 1 bar	0	3	26	110
peanut butter & chocolate, 1 bar	5	1	22	150
strawberry, vanilla yogurt, 1 bar	4	6	53	280
CEREALS/BREAKFAST				
bran, natural wheat, 1 oz	1.5	9	7	47
bran flakes, 1 oz	5	5	19	86
bran flakes, oat, 1 oz	1	4	22	103
chocolate-flavored rice pops, 1 oz	0.5	0.5	25	105
corn flakes, 1 oz	0.5	1	24	97
fruit & fiber flakes, 1 oz	1.5	3	20	96
grapenuts, 1 oz	0	2	22	95
instant oatmeal dry, 1/2 cup	2	3	22	130
muesli, 1 oz	2	2.5	19	106
puffed rice, 1 oz	0	0.5	26	105

FOOD	FAT g	FIBER g	CARB g	ENERGY kcal
puffed wheat, 1 oz	0.5	2.5	20	92
shredded wheat biscuits, 1 oz	1.5	7	48	229
sugar-coated puffed rice, 1 oz	0.5	1.5	23	88

CHARD (see Swiss Chard)

CHEESE

FOOD	FAT g	FIBER g	CARB g	ENERGY kcal
Brie, 1 1/2 oz	12	0	0	141
Camembert, 1 1/2 oz	11	0	0	131
cheddar type, 1 1/2 oz	15	0	0	182
cottage, plain, fat-free, 1/2 cup	0	0	2	96
cottage, plain, whole-fat, 1/2 cup	5	0	3	108
cottage, plain, reduced-fat, 1/2 cup	2	0	4	102
cream, fat-free, 1 oz	0	0	2	30
cream, whole-fat, 1 oz	13	0	0	120
cream, low-fat, 1 oz	5	0	2	65
Danish blue, 1 1/2 oz	12	0	0	141
Edam, 1 1/2 oz	11	0	0	146
Edam-type, reduced-fat, 1 1/2 oz	4	0	0	101
feta, 1 1/2 oz	9	0	0	108
goat, soft, 1 oz	7	0	0.5	80
Gouda, 1 1/2 oz	13	0	0	165
Gruyère, 1 1/2 oz	14	0	0	180

FOOD	FAT g	FIBER g	CARB g	ENERGY kcal
Jarlsberg, 1 1/2 oz	12	0	0	158
mozzarella, 1 1/2 oz	8	0	0	118
Parmesan, 1 1/2 oz	14	0	0	185
processed American, 1 oz	7.5	0	0.5	80
ricotta, 1 oz	4	0	1	58
Roquefort, 1 1/2 oz	14	0	0	165
soy, 1 1/2 oz	12	0	0	128
spread, low-fat, with chives, 1 oz	5	0	1	54
spread, reduced-fat, plain, 1 oz	2	0	1	37
Stilton, blue, 1 1/2 oz	16	0	0	187

CHERRIES

FOOD	FAT g	FIBER g	CARB g	ENERGY kcal
canned in heavy syrup, 1/2 cup	0	1	38	149
raw, 1/2 cup	0	1.5	11	45

CHICKEN

FOOD	FAT g	FIBER g	CARB g	ENERGY kcal
breast, broiled, with skin, 3 oz	5	0	0	149
breast, broiled, without skin, 3 oz	2.5	0	0	127
breast strips, stir-fried, 3 oz	4.5	0	0	138
dark meat, roasted, 3 oz	9.5	0	0	169
drumstick, with skin, (with bone) 3 oz	7	0	0	109
drumstick, meat only, 3 oz	4	0	0	80
light meat, roasted, 3 oz	3.5	0	0	132

FOOD	FAT g	FIBER g	CARB g	ENERGY kcal
portion, fried, dark meat, skin & bone, 3 oz	7	0	0	108
portion, fried, white meat, skin & bone, 3 oz	4	0	0	120
CHICKPEAS				
canned, 1/2 cup	1	5	27	143
CHICORY				
raw, 1 cup	0	2	16	66
CHILE PEPPERS				
hot green or red, raw, 1 each	0	1	4	18
jalapeno, 1 each	0	0	1	4
powder, 1 tsp	1	0	0	0
CHIVES				
fresh, 2 tbsp	0	1	2	12
CHOCOLATE				
coated malted milk balls, 1 oz	8	1	18	141
coated raisins, 1 oz	4	1	19	111
dark, 1 oz	9	3	17	153
expresso beans, 1 oz	7	1	16	128
milk, 1 oz	9	1	17	153
white, 1 oz	9	0	16	162

FOOD	FAT g	FIBER g	CARB g	ENERGY kcal
CHUTNEY, PICKLES & RELISHES				
dill pickle, 1, 4-inch long	0	2	6	24
mango chutney, oily, 1 oz	3	0	14	81
sweet pickle, 1 each, 2½-inch long	0	0	5	18
COCOA				
unsweetened powder, 1 tbsp	1	2	3	12
COLLARD GREENS				
curly, boiled, ½ cup	1	2	1	16
COOKIES				
animal crackers, 1	0	0	1	6
butter, 1	1	0	3	23
chocolate chip, 1 small	4	0.5	9	69
crème-filled chocolate sandwich, 1	2	0	7	47
fig bar, 1	1	1	11	56
oatmeal, 1	2	0	10	61
peanut butter, 1	4	0	9	72
shortbread, 1	4	0	10	75
sugar, 1	3	0	10	72
vanilla wafer, 1	1	0	4	28

FOOD	FAT g	FIBER g	CARB g	ENERGY kcal
CORN				
cob, whole, boiled, 1 ear	1.5	2.5	12	66
kernels, canned, 1/2 cup	1	2	15	66
kernels, frozen, 1/2 cup	1	2	17	72
COUSCOUS				
cooked, 1/2 cup	0	1.5	21	101
CRACKERS				
100% stoned ground wheat, 5 pieces	3	2	14	89
cheese, 5 pieces	1	0	3	25
honey graham, 1 piece	1	0	6	30
melba toast rounds, 5 pieces	0	1	11	59
oyster, 5 each, 5 pieces	1	0	4	22
rye wafers, 1 piece	0	3	9	37
saltine, 5 pieces	2	0	11	65
thin wheat, 5 pieces	2	0	6	47
water, 5 pieces	0	1	10	44
CRANBERRY				
juice, 3/4 cup	0	0	27	41
raw, 1 cup	0	2	1	7
sauce, 1 oz	0	0	11	41

FOOD	FAT g	FIBER g	CARB g	ENERGY kcal
CREAM				
half & half, 2 tbsp	3	0	1	39
heavy, 2 tbsp	11	0	1	103
light, 2 tbsp	9	0	1	87
UHT, spray can, 2 tbsp	10	0	2	100
CROISSANT				
plain, 1 large	14	2	31	272
chocolate-filled, 1	12	1.5	23	216
CUCUMBER				
raw, 1 cup	0	1	3	14
CUSTARD				
powder, with whole milk, 1/2 cup	5	0	23	162
powder, with reduced-fat milk, 1/2 cup	4	0	24	149
ready-made, 4 oz	6	0	27	172

D

FOOD	FAT g	FIBER g	CARB g	ENERGY kcal
DATES				
dried, (with pits) 3 each	0	2	18	68
DESSERTS & PUDDINGS				
apple pie, 1/8 pie	14	2	43	296

FOOD	FAT g	FIBER g	CARB g	ENERGY kcal
banana cream pie, 1/8 pie	20	1	47	387
banana split with whipped cream	65	1	124	1089
bread pudding, 1/2 cup	8	1	31	219
cobbler, apple, 3 x 3-inch slice	6	2	35	199
cobbler, peach, 3 x 3-inch slice	6	2	36	203
chocolate mousse, 1/2 cup	34	0	33	447
crème caramel, 1/2 cup	4	0	25	150
fried fruit pie, individual, 5 x 3 3/4-inch	21	3	55	404
frozen mousse, fat-free, 3 oz	0	1	21	72
instant dessert, with skim milk, 1/2 cup	0	0	29	130
instant dessert, with whole milk, 1/2 cup	4	0	30	169
lemon meringue pie, 1/8 pie	14	1	41	301
rice/tapioca (skim milk), 1/2 cup	0	0	29	140
rice/tapioca (whole milk) pudding, 1/2 cup	3	2	21	130
DIPS & SPREADS				
bean, 1 oz	1	0	5	32
black bean, 1 oz	0	1	5	28

FOOD	FAT g	FIBER g	CARB g	ENERGY kcal
guacamole (avocado), 1 oz	4	1	2	43
hummus, 1 oz	3	2	4	47
onion sour cream, 1 oz	6	0	2	63
peanut butter, 1 tbsp	8	1	3	95
salsa, 1 oz	0	0	1	5
DOUGHNUT				
cake, 1	11	2	37	252
glazed, 1	13	2	28	238
jelly, 1	16	1	33	289
DRESSINGS				
(see also Mayonnaise)				
blue cheese, 1 tbsp	8	0	1	77
caesar (oil/vinegar/cheese),				
1 tbsp	7	0	1	69
fat-free, any, 1 tbsp	0	0	1	75
Italian (oil/vinegar/lemon juice),				
1 tbsp	10.5	0	0.6	89
low-fat, any, 1 tbsp	0.5	0	0	82
oil & lemon, 1 tbsp	10.5	0	1.5	89
ranch, 1 tbsp	8	0	0.5	75
thousand island, 1 tbsp	11	0	0.5	97

FOOD	FAT g	FIBER g	CARB g	ENERGY kcal
thousand island, reduced calorie, 1 tbsp	4.5	0	2	48
vinaigrette (balsamic or wine vinegar),1 tbsp	2.5	0	2	29
yogurt-based, 1 tbsp	5	0	1	50
DRIED FRUIT				
currants, 1/4 cup	0	2	27	102
mixed fruit, 1/4 cup	0	2	25	97
raisins, 1/4 cup	0	1	29	109
DUCK				
roasted, meat only, 3 oz	9	0	0	163
roasted, with fat & skin, 3 oz	33	0	0	364

E

EGG				
egg, whole, 1 medium	5	0	0	68
fried in vegetable oil, 1 medium	11	0	0	121
large egg white only, raw	0	0	0	17
large egg yolk only, raw	5	0	0	59
omelet, plain, 5 oz	20	17	0	229

FOOD	FAT g	FIBER g	CARB g	ENERGY kcal
scrambled with milk & butter,				
1 large	7	0	1	101
EGGPLANT				
cooked & drained, 1/2 cup	1	0	3	14
raw, 1 cup, 82 g	2	2	5	21
ENDIVE				
raw, 1 cup	0	2	2	9

F

FOOD	FAT g	FIBER g	CARB g	ENERGY kcal
FALAFEL				
deep-fried, 21/4-inch patty	3	1	5	57
FAST FOOD/TAKEOUT				
breaded chicken sandwich, 1	23	2	66	582
chicken breast, deep-fried,				
1 piece, 3 oz	8	0	3	170
chicken nuggets, deep-fried,				
3 oz	13	1	13	200
chicken strips, 1 serving	32	5	86	749
corn dog, 1	17	1	23	262
fish (e.g. cod) in batter,				
deep-fried, 3 oz	7	0	6	149

FOOD	FAT g	FIBER g	CARB g	ENERGY kcal
frankfurter in bun, plain	15	0	18	242
french fries, medium	15	0	49	350
broiled cheese sandwich	12	2	39	282
broiled chicken sandwich	13	2	31	343
hamburger, 1 large	23	0	25	400
hamburger, with cheese, 1 large	33	0	47	608
milkshake, 1 medium	10	1	60	369
onion rings, 1 medium	5	7	66	331
tater tots, 1 medium	16	3	27	259
FATS & OILS				
(see also Margarines)				
cocoa butter, 1 tbsp	14	0	0	120
lard, 1 tbsp	13	0	0	115
margarine, 1 tbsp	11	0	0	101
margarine, fat-free spread, 1 tbsp	0	0	0	5
oil, any (e.g. vegetable, corn, olive), 1 tbsp	14	0	0	120
FENNEL				
raw, 1 cup	0	3	6	27

FOOD	FAT g	FIBER g	CARB g	ENERGY kcal
FIGS				
dried, 3 figs, 56 g	0	7	37	158
raw, 1 each, 2½-inch diameter	0	2	12	47
FISH & SEAFOOD				
anchovies, 1 oz	7	0	0	83
angler fish, broiled, 3 oz	0.5	0	0	83
angler fish, raw, 3 oz	0.5	0	0	57
bass, 3 oz	2	0	0	86
calamari, in batter, fried, 3 oz	9	0.5	14	168
carp, 3 oz	4	0	0	96
clams, canned, 3 oz	0.5	0	2	66
cod, deep-fried in batter, 3 oz	13	0.5	10	214
cod fillet, baked, 3 oz	1	0	0	83
cod fillet, poached/steamed, 3 oz	1	0	0	81
cod, smoked, poached, 3 oz	1.5	0	0	87
cod, smoked, raw, 3 oz	0.5	0	0	68
crabmeat, canned, 3 oz	0.5	0	0	65
crayfish, raw, meat only, 3 oz	1	0	0	58
cuttlefish, raw, 3 oz	1	0	0	61
Dover sole, raw, 3 oz	1.5	0	0	77
eel, raw, 3 oz	9.5	0	0	84
eel, smoked, 3 oz	11	0	0	144

FOOD	FAT g	FIBER g	CARB g	ENERGY kcal
flounder, raw, 3 oz	1.5	0	0	71
flounder, steamed, 3 oz	2	0	0	87
flounder fillet, broiled, 3 oz	1.5	0	0	83
flounder fillet, raw, 3 oz	1	0	0	68
flounder fillet, steamed, 3 oz	1.5	0	0	79
flying fish, raw, 3 oz	0.5	0	0	74
haddock fillet, broiled, 3 oz	1	0	0	89
haddock fillet, in crumbs, fried, 3 oz	7	0.5	9	135
haddock fillet, raw, 3 oz	0.5	0	0	70
haddock, smoked, steamed, 3 oz	1	0	0	87
halibut, broiled, 3 oz	2	0	0	104
halibut, raw, 3 oz	1.5	0	0	89
herring, dried, salted, 3 oz	6	0	0	145
herring fillet, broiled, 3 oz	10	0	0	156
herring fillet, raw, 1, 3 oz	11	0	0	161
herring, pickled, 3 oz	10	0	0	180
lemon sole, broiled, 3 oz	1.5	0	0	83
lemon sole, broiled, with bones & skin, 3 oz	1	0	0	53
lemon sole, steamed, 3 oz	1	0	0	78

FOOD	FAT g	FIBER g	CARB g	ENERGY kcal
lemon sole, steamed, with bones & skin, 3 oz	0.5	0	0	55
lobster, meat, boiled, 3 oz	1.5	0	0	88
mackerel, broiled, 3 oz	15	0	0	206
mackerel, raw, 3 oz	14	0	0	189
mackerel, smoked, 3 oz	27	0	0	304
mullet, red, broiled, 3 oz	4	0	0	104
mullet, red, raw, 3 oz	3.5	0	0	104
mullet, stripe, broiled, 3 oz	4.5	0	0	129
mullet, striped raw, 3 oz	4.5	0	0	129
mussels, boiled, without shells, 3 oz	2	0	0	89
octopus, raw, 3 oz	1	0	0	71
orange roughy, raw, 3 oz	6	0	0	108
oysters, raw, 6, 3 oz	1	0	3	56
pollack, Alaskan, raw, 3 oz	0.5	0	0	62
pompano, raw, 3 oz	2	0	0	93
red snapper fillet, fried, 3 oz	2	0	0	108
red snapper, raw, 3 oz	1	0	0	77
redfish, raw, 3 oz	2.5	0	0	84
salmon, broiled, 3 oz	11	0	0	185

FOOD	FAT g	FIBER g	CARB g	ENERGY kcal
salmon, canned, meat only, 3 oz	6	0	0	132
salmon, raw, 3 oz	10	0	0	157
salmon, smoked, 3 oz	4	0	0	121
salmon, steamed, 3 oz	10	0	0	167
sardines, canned in brine, 3 oz	3	0	0	48
sardines, canned in oil, 3 oz	4	0	0	62
scallops, steamed, 3 oz	1	0	3	102
shark, raw, 3 oz	1	0	0	88
shrimp, boiled, 3 oz	1	0	0	84
skate, fillet, broiled, 3 oz	0.5	0	0	68
skate, in batter, fried, 3 oz	8.5	0	4	143
squid, raw, 3 oz	1.5	0	1	70
swordfish, broiled, 3 oz	4	0	0	120
swordfish, raw, 3 oz	3.5	0	0	94
trout, brown, raw, 3 oz	3.5	0	0	96
trout, rainbow, raw, 3 oz	4	0	0	108
tuna, canned in oil, 3 oz	8	0	0	163
tuna, canned in spring water, 3 oz	1	0	0	99
tuna, broiled, 3 oz	6	0	0	143
tuna, raw, 3 oz	4	0	0	117

FOOD	FAT g	FIBER g	CARB g	ENERGY kcal
turbot, broiled, 3 oz	3	0	0	105
turbot, raw, 3 oz	3	0	0	82
whiting, raw, 3 oz	0.5	0	0	70
whiting, steamed, 3 oz	1	0	0	78
FLOUR				
arrowroot, 1 cup	0	4	113	457
buckwheat, 1 cup	4	12	85	402
cornmeal, 1 cup	2	10	107	505
carob, 1 cup	1	41	111	225
millet, 1 cup	4	8	104	440
potato, 1 cup	1	9	95	410
rice, 1 cup	2	4	127	578
rye, whole, 1 cup	4	16	80	400
semolina, raw, 1 cup	2.5	4	98	438
soy, whole-fat, 1 cup	30	13	30	559
100% wheat, 1 cup	2.5	9	86	404
wheat, white, bread making, 1 cup	2	4.5	94	426
white all-purpose, 1 cup	1	3	95	455
FRANKFURTER				
all beef cooked, 1 1/2 oz	12	0	1	134
chicken, 1 1/2 oz	8	0	3	109

FOOD	FAT g	FIBER g	CARB g	ENERGY kcal
tofu dog, 1 1/2 oz	3	0	28	61
turkey, 1 1/2 oz	8	0	6	96
FRUIT SALAD/COCKTAIL				
canned in juice, 1/2 cup	0	1	14	55
canned in syrup, 1/2 cup	0	1	23	91

G

GARLIC				
fresh, peeled, 2 cloves	0	0	1	6
powder, 1 tbsp	0	1	6	28
GELATIN				
powder, 1 oz	0	0	0	96
GINGER				
ground, 1 tbsp	0	1	4	19
root, raw, 1 tbsp	0	0	1	4
GOOSE				
roasted, without bones/skin, 3 oz	19	0	0	274
GRAPEFRUIT				
canned in juice, 1/2 cup	0	1	11	46
canned in syrup, 1/2 cup	0	0	14	56

FOOD	FAT g	FIBER g	CARB g	ENERGY kcal
juice, concentrate, unsweetened, 3/4 cup	0	0	18	76
juice, unsweetened, 3/4 cup	0	0	17	72
raw, 1 each, 4-inch diameter	0	3	21	82
GRAPES				
raw, 1 cup	0	1	16	60
GRAVY				
beef, canned, 1 oz	1	0	1	15
brown, dry, 1 tbsp	1	0	4	22
white, prepared, 1 oz	3	0	3	42
GUACAMOLE (see Dips)				
GUAVA				
raw, 1 each	1	5	11	46

H

HAM				
canned, 1 slice, 1 oz	4	0	0	64
dry-cured prosciutto, 1 oz	10	0	0	189
honey roast, 1 oz	4.5	0	<1	126
oak smoked, 1 oz	3	0	<1	104
Parma, 1 oz	10	0	0	187

FOOD	FAT g	FIBER g	CARB g	ENERGY kcal
HONEY				
honeycomb, 1 oz	4	0	21	78
strained, jar, 1 oz	0	0	22	80
HORSERADISH				
raw, 1 tsp	0	0	2	9
sauce, 1 oz	3	0	1	29
HUMMUS (see Dips)				

I

FOOD	FAT g	FIBER g	CARB g	ENERGY kcal
ICE CREAM				
cake cone, with 1/2 cup vanilla, 1	6	0	46	338
chocolate covered bar, 1	23	2	36	339
dairy, vanilla, 1 bar	13	0	15	190
soft scoop, vanilla, 1/2 cup	5	0	22	140
sugar cone, with 1/2 cup vanilla	12	0	20	195
vanilla, in dish, 1/2 cup	12	0	17	178
wafflecone, with 1/2 cup vanilla	17	0	39	318

FOOD	FAT g	FIBER g	CARB g	ENERGY kcal
J				
JAM				
apricot, 1 tsp	0	0	13	48
black currant, reduced sugar, 1 tsp	0	0	10	40
fruit marmalade, 1 tsp	0	0	6	21
reduced sugar, 1 tsp	0	0	3	10
strawberry conserve, high fruit, 1 tsp	0	0	7	29
K				
KIWI FRUIT				
raw, with peel, 1 medium	0	3	14	56
KOHLRABI				
boiled, 1/2 cup	0	1	6	24
raw, 1 cup	0	5	8	36
KUMQUAT				
raw, 1	0	1	3	12

FOOD	FAT g	FIBER g	CARB g	ENERGY kcal
L				
LAMB				
lean, roast, 3 oz	15	0	0	217
cutlets, best end, lean, barbecued, 3 oz	12	0	0	203
cutlets, best end, lean & fat, barbecued, 3 oz	23	0	0	294
leg, roast, lean, 3 oz	7	0	0	162
loin chop, broiled, lean, 3 oz	11	0	0	186
shoulder, roasted, lean, 3 oz	9	0	0	169
LARD (see Fats & Oils)				
LASAGNA (see Ready Meals)				
LEEKS				
boiled, 1/2 cup	0.5	1	1	11
raw, 1 each	0.5	3	3	22
LEMON				
curd, 1 tsp	1	0	9	42
juice, fresh, 1/2 cup	0	0	4	13
raw, 1 each, with peel	0.5	5	3	22
LENTILS				
boiled, 1/2 cup	0	8	20	115

FOOD	FAT g	FIBER g	CARB g	ENERGY kcal
LETTUCE				
frisee/lamb's lettuce/lollo				
rosso, mixed, 1 cup	0	1	2	9
iceberg, 1 cup	0	1	1	7
raddicchio, 1 cup	0	1	1	8
Romaine, 1 cup	0.5	1	1	9
LIME				
juice, fresh, 1/2 cup	0	0	4	16
raw, without peel, 1 each	0	1	7	20
LIVER				
calf, fried, 3 oz	11	0	6	217
chicken, fried, 3 oz	8.5	0	2	166

M

FOOD	FAT g	FIBER g	CARB g	ENERGY kcal
MACARONI (see Pasta)				
MANDARIN (loose-skinned) ORANGES				
mandarin segments, canned				
in juice, 1/2 cup	0	1	12	46
mandarin segments, canned in				
light syrup, 1/2 cup	0	1	20	77
tangerine, raw, peeled, 1	0	2	11	43

FOOD	FAT g	FIBER g	CARB g	ENERGY kcal
MANGO				
canned in syrup, 1/2 cup	0	1	24	87
raw, 1 each	0.5	4	35	135
MAPLE SYRUP				
1 tbsp	0	0	13	53
MARGARINE				
(see Fats & Oils)				
MARMALADE (see Jam)				
MARZIPAN				
1 tbsp	3	0.5	14	81
MATZO				
square, 1 large	0.5	0.5	18	79
MAYONNAISE				
homemade, 1 tbsp	13	0	0	119
prepared, 1 tbsp	12	0	0	104
prepared, reduced-calorie,				
1 tbsp	5	0	1	50
MEAT SUBSTITUTE				
texturized vegetable protein				
(TVP), 1 oz	1	5	7	82
MELON				
cantaloupe-type, 1 cup	0	1.5	7	32

FOOD	FAT g	FIBER g	CARB g	ENERGY kcal
honeydew, 1 cup	0	1.5	11	48
watermelon, 1 cup	0	0.5	8	37
MERINGUE				
shell, plain	0	0	8	30
MILK				
buttermilk, 8 fl oz	8	0	12	99
condensed, whole-fat, sweetened, 8 fl oz	27	0	166	982
dried skim, prepared, 8 fl oz	0	0	12	82
evaporated, whole-fat, 8 fl oz	54	0	26	338
goat, 8 fl oz	10	0	11	168
reduced-fat, 8 fl oz	5	0	12	122
skim, 8 fl oz	0	0	12	86
soy, plain, 8 fl oz	7	0	14	160
soy, plain, low-fat, 8 fl oz	2	0	16	100
whole, 8 fl oz	8	0	11	150
MISO				
1 tbsp	1	1	5	35
MIXED FRUIT				
(see Dried Fruit)				
MIXED VEGETABLES				
frozen, boiled, 1/2 cup	0	4	12	54

FOOD	FAT g	FIBER g	CARB g	ENERGY kcal
MOLASSES				
1 tbsp	0	0	10	40
MULBERRIES				
raw, 1 cup	0	2	11	50
MUSHROOMS				
button, cooked, 1/2 cup	0	0	2	14
button, raw, 1 cup	0	1	4	24
Chinese, enokii, raw, 1	0	0	0	2
oyster, raw, 1 large	1	4	9	55
portabello, raw, 2 1/2 oz	0	1	3	25
shitake, cooked, 2 1/2 oz	0	0	10	40
MUSTARD				
American, 1 tsp	0	0	0	3
English, powder, 1 tsp	1	0	1	14
French, 1 tsp	0	0	0	4
whole-grain, retail, 1 tsp	1.5	0	1	20

N

FOOD	FAT g	FIBER g	CARB g	ENERGY kcal
NECTARINE				
raw, 1	0	3.5	14	60

FOOD	FAT g	FIBER g	CARB g	ENERGY kcal
NOODLES				
egg, boiled, 1/2 cup	1	1.5	21	99
plain, boiled, 1/2 cup	0	1	20	99
rice, white, cooked, 1/2 cup	0	1	22	96
NUTS				
almonds, shelled, 1 oz	15	4	2	166
Brazil, shelled, 1 oz	19	2	1	189
cashew nuts, roasted/salted, 1 oz	14	3	6	170
chestnuts, peeled, 1 oz	1	2	10	48
hazel, shelled, 1 oz	17	2	2	181
peanuts, dry roasted, 1 oz	13	2	3	165
peanuts, roasted/salted, 1 oz	15	2	2	169
pecans, shelled, 1 oz	21	2	2	207
pistachios, roasted/salted, 1 oz	17	3	3	168
walnuts, shelled, 6 halves, 1 oz	20	2	1	193

O

OILS (see Fats & Oils)

FOOD	FAT g	FIBER g	CARB g	ENERGY kcal
OKRA				
boiled, 1/2 cup	0	2	6	26
fried, 1/2 cup	6	1	7	88
OLIVES				
in brine, pitted, 1 oz	5	0	2	51
in brine, with pits, 1 oz	3	1	2	33
ONION				
boiled, 1/2 cup	0	2	7	29
pickled, 1/2 cup	0	1	4	17
raw, 1 medium	0	3	14	60
ORANGE				
juice, fresh squeezed, 3/4 cup	0	0	19	83
juice, unsweetened, 3/4 cup	0	0	20	84
raw, 1 medium, peeled	0	3	15	62

P

FOOD	FAT g	FIBER g	CARB g	ENERGY kcal
PANCAKE/CREPE				
crepe without filling, 1	6	0	11	115
pancake, plain, 6-inch diameter	2	1	28	149

FOOD	FAT g	FIBER g	CARB g	ENERGY kcal
PARSNIP				
boiled, 1/2 cup	1	3.5	10	52
PASSION FRUIT				
raw, 1 each	0	2	4	17
PASTA				
buckwheat pasta, cooked, 1/2 cup	0.5	0	17	81
macaroni, boiled, 1/2 cup	0	1	20	99
potato gnocchi, fresh, cooked, 1/2 cup	7	1	17	134
ravioli, fresh, cheese, 1/2 cup	6	0	16	140
spaghetti, cooked, 1/2 cup	0	1	20	99
PASTA SAUCE				
alfredo, 1/2 cup	15	1	7	200
four cheese, 1/2 cup	4	2	8	82
pesto, 1/2 cup	57	4	8	620
tomato & basil, 1/2 cup	0	1	9	43
PASTRY				
filo, raw, 1 sheet (generous 1/2 oz)	0	0	12	60
puff, baked, 1 oz	11	0	13	158

FOOD	FAT g	FIBER g	CARB g	ENERGY kcal
PATE				
liver, 1 oz	8	0	0	90
chicken with vegetables, 1 oz	1	0	0	42
PEACH				
canned in juice, 1/2 cup	0	2	14	55
canned in syrup, 1/2 cup	0	1	14	71
dried halves, 3 each	0	3	24	93
raw, with skin, 1 medium	0	2.5	8	36
PEAR				
canned in juice, 1/2 cup	0	2	16	63
canned in syrup, 1/2 cup	0	2	26	98
dried halves, 2 each	0	3	24	92
raw, with peel, 1	1	4	25	98
PEAS				
frozen, boiled, 1/2 cup	1	6	8	55
raw, shelled, 1/2 cup	0	4	10	59
split, dried, boiled, 1/2 cup	0	8	21	116
PEPPERS (see Bell Peppers)				
PINEAPPLE				
canned in juice, 1/2 cup	0	1	20	76
canned in syrup, 1/2 cup	0	1	26	99
dried, 1/4 cup	0	0	5	19

FOOD	FAT g	FIBER g	CARB g	ENERGY kcal
juice, 3/4 cup	0	0	26	105
raw, 1 slice, without skin,				
3 x 3/4-inch	0	1	8	30
PLUMS				
canned in juice, 1/2 cup	0	1	19	73
canned in syrup, 1/2 cup	0	1	30	115
dried, 3 each	0	2	16	60
raw, with pit, 1 small	0.5	1	10	40
PORK				
Canadian bacon, sliced, lean				
only, broiled, 3 oz	2	0	0	53
leg, roasted, lean only, 3 oz	6	0	0	157
loin chop, broiled, lean only, 3 oz	10	0	0	194
skins, BBQ flavor, 1 oz	9	0	0	153
POTATO				
baked, flesh/skin, 1 medium	0.5	1	57	245
boiled, 1/2 cup	0	1	16	67
French fries, oven-baked, 1 oz	1.5	2	23	110
mashed, with butter & milk,				
1/2 cup	4	2	18	111
new, boiled, with skin, 1/2 cup	0	1	20	80

FOOD	FAT g	FIBER g	CARB g	ENERGY kcal
PRUNES				
canned in syrup, 1/2 cup	0	4	3	123
dried, 3 each	0	2	16	60
stewed, 1/2 cup	0	8	35	133
juice, 3/4 cup	0	2	34	136
PUMPKIN				
boiled, 1/2 cup	0.5	0.5	2	16

Q

FOOD	FAT g	FIBER g	CARB g	ENERGY kcal
QUICHE				
Lorraine, (cream, bacon, cheese), 1/8 piece	41	1	25	526

R

FOOD	FAT g	FIBER g	CARB g	ENERGY kcal
RABBIT				
roasted, 3 oz	7	0	0	168
RADISH				
red, raw, 10 radishes	0	0.5	1	6
RAISINS (see Dried Fruit)				

FOOD	FAT g	FIBER g	CARB g	ENERGY kcal
RASPBERRIES				
canned in syrup, 1/2 cup	0	6	28	112
frozen, raw, 1 cup	0.5	7	5	26
raw, 1 cup	0.5	8.5	6	32
READY-TO-COOK FOOD				
bean & cheese burrito, 1	9	6	66	390
beef burrito, 1	10	1	29	262
beef enchiladas with rice & beans, frozen meal	30	8	68	634
beef soft taco, 1	10	2	20	230
burger, vegetarian, 1 3/4 oz	2	1	2	52
cannelloni, spinach & ricotta, 15 3/4 oz	35	2	58	662
cheese enchilada with rice & cheese, frozen meal	15	5	48	376
chicken burrito, 1	22	9	66	580
chicken chow mein, 12 oz	7	7	49	353
chicken kiev, 5 oz	35	1	14	427
chicken kiev, reduced-fat, 5 oz	20	1	16	319
chicken pie, individual, baked, 4 1/2 oz	23	3	32	374
chicken soft taco, 1	7	2	21	200

FOOD	FAT g	FIBER g	CARB g	ENERGY kcal
chile con carne, 7¾ oz	19	7	18	332
chow mein, 3½ oz	3	1	16	119
cod fillet, breaded, 1 fillet, 6 oz	13	3	24	304
cod fish cake, 3¼ oz	8	1	15	168
corned beef hash, canned, 7 oz	18	0	12	328
egg fried rice, 3½ oz	2	1	25	149
falafel, 6 each, 3 oz	7	7	16	200
fish sticks, breaded, 3 oz	11	1	18	205
garlic bread, half baguette, 3 oz	16	2	41	342
garlic bread, half baguette, reduced-fat, 3¼ oz	8	2	41	263
gefilte fish balls, 6 pieces, 3½ oz	4	1	12	140
grape leaves, stuffed (lamb & rice), 3 rolls	13	2	7	167
hash browns, 3½ oz	7	0	24	174
lasagna, meat, 3½ oz	9	1	10	161
lasagna, vegetable, 3½ oz	5	1	14	212
macaroni & cheese, prepared, ½ cup	7	1	15	151
macaroni cheese, canned, 7 oz	10	1	20	191
noodle, Thai-style, 3½ oz	6	1	16	142

FOOD	FAT g	FIBER g	CARB g	ENERGY kcal
pasta with meatballs in tomato sauce canned, 1/2 cup	5	3	14	117
pizza, deep-dish, pepperoni, 6 oz	23	3	60	485
pizza, deep-dish, sausage, 6 oz	24	0	49	471
pizza, thin, Canadian bacon, 6 oz	21	2	35	415
pizza, thin & crispy, cheese, 6 oz	19	2	48	440
pizza, vegetable, 6 oz	11	3	44	332
ramen noodles, instant beef or chicken, 1 each	1	1	29	151
ravioli, meat, canned in tomato sauce, 8 oz	5	3	34	213
shrimp cocktail, 3 oz	1	2	8	81
spaghetti & meatballs, canned, 8 oz	8	2	32	236
spaghetti rings in tomato sauce, can, 8 oz	8	1	26	223
spring roll, vegetable, 1, 2 1/4 oz	6	1	9	113
sweet & sour pork, canned, 8 oz	26	7	141	721

FOOD	FAT g	FIBER g	CARB g	ENERGY kcal
tortellini, fresh, meat, 3 oz	7	1	15	167
tortellini, spinach & ricotta, 3 oz	6	1	18	162

RED CURRANTS

jelly, 1 tsp	0	0	4	17

RHUBARB

frozen, cooked with sugar,				
½ cup	0	2	37	139
raw, 1 cup	0	2	6	26

RICE

basmati, boiled, ½ cup	0	0	15	79
brown, boiled, ½ cup	0.5	1	22	102
red (wild), cooked, ½ cup	1	1.5	31	137
white, minute rice, boiled,				
½ cup	0	0	17	80
white, polished, boiled, ½ cup	1	1	31	136

RICE CAKE

plain, 1 piece	0	0	6	28

RUTABAGA

boiled, ½ cup	0	2	7	33
raw, 1 cup	0	4	11	50

FOOD	FAT g	FIBER g	CARB g	ENERGY kcal

S

SAUCES

FOOD	FAT g	FIBER g	CARB g	ENERGY kcal
brown, espagnole, prepared, 1 oz	3	0	14	89
cheese, prepared, 1 oz	4	0	2	56
hollandaise, 1 oz	13	0	0	121
ketchup, bottled, 1 tbsp	0	0	4	16
white, whole milk, 1 oz	2	0	1	23
Worcestershire, 1 tbsp	0	0	3	11

SAUSAGE

FOOD	FAT g	FIBER g	CARB g	ENERGY kcal
beef, fried or broiled, 1 oz	8	0	1	88
bratwurst, 3 oz	19	0	2	224
chorizo, 1 oz	21	0	1	258
liverwurst, 1 oz	15	0.5	5	194
mortadella, 1 oz	26	0	<1	285
salami, 1 slice, 1 oz	13	0	0.5	137
salami stick, 1 oz	13	0	0.5	148
vegetarian, soy protein, cooked, 1 oz	12	1	7	214

SCALLIONS

FOOD	FAT g	FIBER g	CARB g	ENERGY kcal
raw, 1 cup	1	2.5	3	20

FOOD	FAT g	FIBER g	CARB g	ENERGY kcal
SEEDS				
poppy, 1 oz	13	3	7	151
pumpkin, 1 oz	12	1	4	148
sesame, 1 oz	14	4	7	160
sunflower, 1 oz	14	3	7	165
SNACKS				
banana chips, 1 oz	9	1.5	17	143
cheese puffs, 1 oz	10	1	15	160
corn chips (tortilla), 1 oz	8	1	17	140
pretzels, 1 oz	1	1	22	108
shoestring French fried potato chips, 1 oz	2	1	7	43
trail mix, 1 oz	8	1	13	131
SOFT DRINKS				
cola type, canned, 12 fl oz	0	0	39	152
diet (light) cola, canned, 12 fl oz	0	0	0	1
diet (light) lemonade, canned, 12 fl oz	0	0	16	65
ginger ale, canned, 12 fl oz	0	0	32	124
iced tea, sweetened, canned 12 fl oz	0	0	27	98
lemonade, canned, 12 fl oz	0	0	45	180

FOOD	FAT g	FIBER g	CARB g	ENERGY kcal
SOUPS				
beef broth, ready-to-serve, 1 cup	1	0	0	16
black bean, 1 cup	1.5	4	20	116
chicken & rice, prepared, 1 cup	2	0	7	251
chicken broth, ready-to-serve, 1 cup	1	0	1	39
chicken noodle, prepared, 1 cup	2	0	9	75
clam chowder Manhattan, as prepared, 1 cup	2	0	12	77
clam chowder New England, prepared with milk, 1 cup	7	0	17	163
cream of asparagus, as prepared with milk, 1 cup	8	0	16	161
cream of celery, prepared with milk, 1 cup	10	0	15	165
cream of chicken prepared with milk, 1 cup	11	0	15	116
cream of mushroom, as prepared with milk, 1 cup	14	0	15	203
cream of potato, prepared with milk, 1 cup	6	0	17	148

FOOD	FAT g	FIBER g	CARB g	ENERGY kcal
cream of tomato prepared				
with milk, 1 cup	6	0	22	160
french onion, prepared, 1 cup	2	0	8	57
gazpacho, ready-to-serve, 1 cup	2	0	1	57
lentil soup, prepared, 1 cup	2	7	22	140
minestrone, prepared, 1 cup	2.5	1	11	82
split pea with ham, prepared				
with water, 1 cup	4	2	28	190
SPINACH				
fresh, boiled, 1/2 cup	1	3	1	17
frozen, boiled, 1/2 cup	0.5	1.5	0	10
raw, 1 cup	0.5	2	1	14
SQUASH				
acorn, baked, 1/2 cup	0	4.5	13	57
butternut, baked, 1/2 cup	0	3	11	41
spaghetti, baked, 1/2 cup	0	1	5	21
STAR FRUIT (Carambola)				
raw, 1	0.5	2	7	32
STRAWBERRIES				
raw, 1 cup	0	3	9	41

FOOD	FAT g	FIBER g	CARB g	ENERGY kcal
STUFFING				
corn bread, 1/2 cup	8	1	19	160
herb bread, 1/2 cup	9	1	20	170
SUGAR				
white granulated, 1 tsp	0	0	4	16
SUGAR SNAP PEAS				
boiled, 1/2 cup	0	2	7	40
frozen, boiled, 1/2 cup	0	2	8	38
raw, 1 cup	0	5	15	76
SWEETCORN (see Corn)				
SWEET POTATO				
boiled, 1 medium potato	0.5	2.5	33	96
raw, 1 medium	0.5	4	32	136
SWISS CHARD				
cooked, 1/2 cup	0	2	3	18
raw, 1 cup	0	0.5	1	6

T

FOOD	FAT g	FIBER g	CARB g	ENERGY kcal
TAHINI				
1 tbsp	9	1	2	91

FOOD	FAT g	FIBER g	CARB g	ENERGY kcal
TANGERINE				
(see Mandarin Oranges)				
TAPIOCA				
raw, 1/2 cup	0	1	67	272
TOFU				
extra firm, 4 oz	2	0	2	62
silken, 4 oz	3	0	3	62
silken, light, 4 oz	1	0	1	42
TOMATO				
cherry, raw, 1 cup	0	0	6	23
juice, 1/2 cup	0	1	4	19
peeled, whole, canned, 1/2 cup	0	1	5	25
paste, 1 tbsp	0	1	3	13
raw, 1 medium	0	1	6	26
sun-dried, 1 oz	1	3	16	73
sun-dried in oil, 1 oz	4	2	7	60
TORTILLA (see Breads)				
TURKEY				
breast fillet, broiled, 3 oz	2	0	0	133
drumstick, roasted, with				
skin & bone, 3 oz	5	0	0	135
roasted, dark meat, no skin, 3 oz	3	0	0	127

FOOD	FAT g	FIBER g	CARB g	ENERGY kcal
roasted, light meat, no skin,				
3 oz	1	0	0	114
roll, 1 slice, 1 oz	1	0	0	16
smoked, 1 oz	0.5	0	0	31
TURNIP				
boiled, 1/2 cup	0	1.5	1.5	9
raw, diced, 1 cup	0	1	8	36

V

VEAL				
scallop/cutlet, in breadcrumbs,				
fried, 3 oz	14	0	7	228
scallop, meat, no coating,				
fried, 3 oz	4	0	0	156
shoulder roast with bone, lean,				
roasted, 3 oz	5	0	0	169
VENISON				
roasted, 3 oz	4	0	0	279
VINEGAR				
all varieties, 1 tbsp	0	0	0	4

FOOD	FAT g	FIBER g	CARB g	ENERGY kcal
W				
WAFFLES				
plain, 1 each, 7-inch diameter	11	1	25	218
WATER CHESTNUTS				
canned, 1/2 cup	0	2	9	35
raw, 1 cup	0.5	2	12	57
WATERCRESS				
fresh, 1 oz	0.5	1	0	7
Y				
YAM				
cooked, 1/2 cup	0	2.5	22	90
raw, 1 medium	0	0.5	22	92
YEAST				
bakers, compressed, 2/3 oz	0	1	3	18
dried, 1 tsp	0	1	2	12
YOGURT				
fat-free, plain, 8 oz	0	0	17	127
fruit-on-bottom, all flavors, 8 oz	3	1	46	240

FOOD	FAT g	FIBER g	CARB g	ENERGY kcal
low-fat, fruit, 1 cup	3	0	42	225
low-fat, plain, 1 cup	4	0	16	143
nonfat, fruit with low-calorie sweetener, 1 cup	0	1	18	115
very low-fat, plain, 8 oz	4	0	16	144
whole milk, plain, 1 cup	7	0	11	138

Z

ZUCCHINI

cooked, 1/2 cup	0	1.5	4	14
raw, 1 cup	0	1.5	4	18

RECIPES:
DELICIOUS BREAKFASTS, LUNCHES, DINNERS, AND DESSERTS

YOGURT WITH HONEY, NUTS & BLUEBERRIES

Serves 4

Ingredients
3 tbsp honey
scant ¾ cup mixed unsalted nuts
8 tbsp plain yogurt
scant 1 cup fresh blueberries

Nutritional Fact
Excellent for balancing blood sugar, blueberries are, therefore, a good food with which to start the day.

Serving Analysis
- Calories 239
- Protein 4.3 g
- Carbohydrate 24 g
- Sugars 19.4 g
- Fat 15.6 g
- Saturates 2.7 g

1 Heat the honey in a small pan over medium heat, add the nuts, and stir until they are well coated. Remove from the heat and let cool slightly.

2 Divide the yogurt between 4 serving bowls, then spoon over the nut mixture and blueberries.

MEXICAN EGGS

Serves 4

Ingredients
8 large eggs
2 tbsp milk
freshly ground black pepper
1 tsp olive oil
1 red bell pepper, deseeded and
thinly sliced
1/2 fresh red chile pepper
1 fresh chorizo sausage, skinned
and sliced
4 tbsp chopped fresh cilantro
To serve
4 slices toasted whole-wheat bread

Nutritional Fact
A good protein breakfast helps to
sustain good blood-sugar levels
throughout the day.
Serving Analysis
• Calories 279
• Protein 15.8 g
• Carbohydrate 4.9 g
• Sugars 3.9 g
• Fat 21.8 g
• Saturates 6.3 g

1 Beat the eggs, milk, and pepper to taste in a large bowl. Set aside.

2 Heat the oil in a nonstick skillet over medium heat, add the red bell
pepper and chile and cook, stirring frequently, for 5 minutes, or until
the red bell pepper is soft and browned in places. Add the chorizo and
cook until just browned. Transfer to a warmed plate and set aside.

3 Return the skillet to the heat, add the egg mixture, and cook to a soft
scramble. Add the chorizo mixture, stir to combine, and sprinkle over
the cilantro. Serve at once on toasted whole-wheat bread.

BIRCHER GRANOLA

Serves 4

Ingredients
scant 1³/4 cups rolled oats
1 cup apple juice
1 apple, grated
¹/2 cup plain yogurt
scant ³/4 cup blackberries
2 plums, pitted and sliced
2 tbsp honey

Nutritional Fact
Oats release their sugars very slowly, making them a good breakfast food.

Serving Analysis
• Calories 285
• Protein 8.4 g
• Carbohydrate 56 g
• Sugars 25.5 g
• Fat 4.2 g
• Saturates 1.1 g

1 Put the oats and apple juice into a mixing bowl and combine well. Cover and let chill overnight.

2 To serve, stir the apple and yogurt into the soaked oats and divide between 4 serving bowls. Top with the blackberries and plums and drizzle with the honey.

BAKED MUSHROOMS

Serves 4

Ingredients
2 tbsp olive oil
8 portobello mushrooms
3/4 cup finely chopped white mushrooms
2 garlic cloves, crushed
4 slices lean cooked ham, finely chopped
2 tbsp finely chopped fresh parsley
pepper
To serve
4 slices rye bread

Nutritional Fact
Parsley is a good stress tonic that helps to keep blood-sugar levels manageable.

Serving Analysis
• Calories 124
• Protein 6.6 g
• Carbohydrate 4 g
• Sugars 1.2 g
• Fat 9.7 g
• Saturates 0.8 g

1 Preheat the oven to 375 °F/190 °C. Brush a baking sheet with a little of the oil. Arrange the portobello mushrooms, cup-side up, on the baking sheet.

2 Mix the white mushrooms, garlic, ham, and parsley together in a bowl.

3 Divide the ham mixture between the portobello mushroom cups. Drizzle with the remaining oil and season with pepper to taste.

4 Bake in the preheated oven for 10 minutes, then serve at once with rye bread.

WINTER WARMER RED LENTIL SOUP

Serves 6

Ingredients

generous 1 cup dried red split lentils
1 red onion, diced
2 large carrots, sliced
1 celery stalk, sliced
1 parsnip, diced
1 garlic clove, crushed
5 cups vegetable stock
2 tsp paprika
freshly ground black pepper
1 tbsp snipped fresh chives, to garnish

To serve

6 tbsp low-fat mascarpone cheese
(optional)
crusty whole-wheat or white bread

Nutritional Fact

Lentils contain good levels of B vitamins, which are thought to stop the accumulation of a substance called homocysteine that can build up in the body and cause damage to the heart.

Serving Analysis

- Calories 87
- Protein 4.4g
- Carbohydrate 18g
- Sugars 5g
- Fat 0.4g
- Saturates 0.07g

1 Put the lentils, onion, vegetables, garlic, stock, and paprika into a large pan. Bring to a boil and boil rapidly for 10 minutes. Reduce the heat, cover, and let simmer for 20 minutes, or until the lentils and vegetables are tender.

2 Let the soup cool slightly, then puree in small batches in a food processor or blender. Process until the mixture is smooth.

3 Return the soup to the pan and heat through thoroughly. Season with pepper to taste.

4 To serve, ladle the soup into warmed bowls and swirl in a tablespoonful of mascarpone cheese, if desired. Sprinkle the chives over the soup to garnish and serve at once with crusty bread.

SPEEDY BROCCOLI SOUP

Serves 6

Ingredients

2 medium heads of broccoli, about 12 oz/350 g
1 leek, sliced
1 celery stalk, sliced
1 garlic clove, crushed
2 1/3 cups diced potatoes
4 cups vegetable stock
1 bay leaf
freshly ground black pepper

To serve

crusty bread or toasted croutons

Nutritional Fact

Broccoli is a source of vitamins B3 and B5, both of which are thought to raise good cholesterol levels in the blood, and, therefore, help to balance good and bad cholesterol levels.

Serving Analysis

- Calories 140
- Protein 5.6 g
- Carbohydrate 29 g
- Sugars 3.6 g
- Fat 1.3 g
- Saturates 0.27 g

1 Cut the broccoli into florets and set aside. Cut the thicker broccoli stalks into 1/2-inch/1-cm dice and put into a large pan with the leek, celery, garlic, potato, stock, and bay leaf. Bring to a boil, then reduce the heat, cover, and let simmer for 15 minutes

2 Add the broccoli florets to the soup and return to a boil. Reduce the heat, cover, and let simmer for an additional 3–5 minutes, or until the potato and broccoli stalks are tender.

3 Remove from the heat and let the soup cool slightly. Remove and discard the bay leaf. Puree the soup, in small batches in a food processor or blender until smooth.

4 Return the soup to the pan and heat through thoroughly. Season with pepper to taste. Ladle the soup into warmed bowls and serve at once with crusty bread or toasted croutons.

BAKED LEMON COD

Serves 4

Ingredients

1/3 cucumber
2 celery stalks
4 thick cod fillets, about 5 oz/140 g each
1 tbsp chopped fresh parsley
grated rind and juice of 1 lemon
freshly ground black pepper

To serve

lemon wedges, to garnish
boiled new potatoes, lightly cooked
seasonal vegetables, or salads

Nutritional Fact

White fish, such as cod and flounder, is low in saturated fat and high in protein that is essential for healthy building and repair of the body's cells.

Serving Analysis

• Calories 121
• Protein 25 g
• Carbohydrate 2.6 g
• Sugars 1.2 g
• Fat 1.3 g
• Saturates 0.02 g

1 Preheat the oven to 400 °F/200 °C. Cut the cucumber and celery into long fine sticks and sprinkle over the bottom of an ovenproof dish that is large enough to fit the cod fillets in a single layer.

2 Arrange the cod fillets on the cucumber and celery and sprinkle the parsley, lemon rind, and juice over the fillets. Season with pepper. Cover the dish with an ovenproof lid or foil and bake in the preheated oven for about 20 minutes, depending on the thickness of the fillets, until the flesh turns white and flakes easily.

3 Transfer the fish to a warmed serving plate with the cucumber and celery and spoon over the cooking juices. Garnish with lemon wedges and serve at once with boiled new potatoes, seasonal vegetables, or salads.

BEEF BOURGUIGNON

Serves 4

Ingredients

14 oz/400 g lean beef
2 low-salt lean smoked Canadian
bacon slices
12 shallots, peeled
1 garlic clove, crushed
3¼ cups sliced button mushrooms
1¼ cups red wine
scant 2 cups beef stock
2 bay leaves
2 tbsp chopped fresh thyme
6 tablespoons cornstarch
generous ⅓ cup cold water
freshly ground black pepper
To serve
boiled brown or white rice
lightly cooked seasonal vegetables

Nutritional Fact

Choosing brown rice instead of white can help to increase your intake of insoluble fiber and B vitamins and clean toxins out of your system.

Serving Analysis

• Calories 376
• Protein 35 g
• Carbohydrate 20 g
• Sugars 1.6 g
• Fat 11 g
• Saturates 4.1 g

1 Trim any visible fat from the beef and bacon and cut the meat into bite-size pieces. Put the meat into a large pan with the shallots, garlic, mushrooms, wine, stock, bay leaves, and 1 tablespoon of the thyme. Bring to a boil, then reduce the heat, cover, and let simmer for 50 minutes, or until the meat and shallots are tender.

2 Blend the cornstarch with the water in a small bowl and stir into the casserole. Return to a boil, stirring constantly, and cook until the casserole thickens. Reduce the heat and let simmer for an additional 5 minutes. Season with pepper to taste.

3 Remove and discard the bay leaves. Transfer the beef bourguignon to a warmed casserole dish and sprinkle over the remaining thyme. Serve with boiled rice and seasonal vegetables.

STICKY LIME CHICKEN

Serves 4

Ingredients

4 part-boned, skinless chicken breasts, about 5 oz/140 g each
grated rind and juice of 1 lime
1 tbsp honey
1 tbsp olive oil
1 garlic clove, chopped (optional)
1 tbsp chopped fresh thyme
freshly ground black pepper

To serve

boiled new potatoes
lightly cooked seasonal vegetables

Nutritional Fact

Removing the skin from the chicken gets rid of most of the saturated fat.

Serving Analysis

- Calories 203
- Protein 32.5 g
- Carbohydrate 5.3 g
- Sugars 4.4 g
- Fat 5.3 g
- Saturates 1 g

1 Preheat the oven to 375 °F/190 °C. Arrange the chicken breasts in a shallow roasting pan.

2 Put the lime rind and juice, honey, oil, garlic, if using, and thyme in a small bowl and combine thoroughly. Spoon the mixture evenly over the chicken breasts and season with pepper.

3 Roast the chicken in the preheated oven, basting every 10 minutes, for 35–40 minutes, or until the chicken is tender and the juices run clear when a skewer is inserted into the thickest part of the meat. If the juices still run pink, return the chicken to the oven and cook for an additional 5 minutes, then retest. As the chicken cooks, the liquid in the pan thickens to form the tasty, sticky coating.

4 Serve with boiled new potatoes and seasonal vegetables.

TUNA & AVOCADO SALAD

Serves 4

Ingredients

2 avocados, pitted, peeled, and cubed
1²/3 cups halved cherry tomatoes
2 red bell peppers, seeded and chopped
1 bunch fresh flat-leaf parsley, chopped
2 garlic cloves, crushed
1 fresh red chile, seeded and finely chopped
juice of ¹/2 lemon
6 tbsp olive oil
pepper
3 tbsp sesame seeds
4 fresh tuna steaks, about 5¹/2 oz/ 150 g each

To serve

8 cooked new potatoes, cubed
arugula leaves, to serve

Nutritional Fact

Avocados are rich in nutrients that can help to protect the eyes against diabetes-related damage.

Serving Analysis

- Calories 785
- Protein 44 g
- Carbohydrate 57 g
- Sugars 7.1 g
- Fat 46 g
- Saturates 3 g

1 Toss the avocados, tomatoes, red bell peppers, parsley, garlic, chile, lemon juice, and 2 tablespoons of the oil together in a large bowl. Season with pepper to taste, cover, and let chill in the refrigerator for 30 minutes. Lightly crush the sesame seeds in a mortar with a pestle. Turn the crushed seeds onto a plate and spread out. Press each tuna steak in turn into the crushed seeds to coat on both sides.

2 Heat 2 tablespoons of the remaining oil in a skillet, add the potatoes, and cook, stirring frequently, for 5–8 minutes, or until crisp and brown. Remove from the skillet and drain on paper towels.

3 Wipe out the skillet, add the remaining oil, and heat over high heat until very hot. Add the tuna steaks and cook for 3–4 minutes on each side. Divide the avocado salad between 4 serving plates and top each with a tuna steak, then sprinkle over the potatoes and a handful of rocket leaves.

TOASTED PINE NUT & VEGETABLE COUSCOUS

Serves 4

Ingredients

generous ¹/₂ cup dried green lentils
6 tablespoons pine nuts
1 tbsp olive oil
1 onion, diced
2 garlic cloves, crushed
2¹/₂ cups sliced zucchini
1¹/₃ cups chopped tomatoes
14 oz/400 g canned artichoke hearts,
drained and cut in half lengthwise
generous 1¹/₄ cups couscous
2 cups vegetable stock
3 tbsp torn fresh basil leaves, plus extra
leaves to garnish
freshly ground black pepper

Nutritional Fact

Pine kernels have beneficial omega-3 oils and polyunsaturated fats. They also contain plant sterols, which are thought to help to regulate cholesterol.

Serving Analysis

- Calories 600
- Protein 17 g
- Carbohydrate 71 g
- Sugars 7.9 g
- Fat 28 g
- Saturates 4 g

1 Put the lentils into a pan with plenty of cold water and boil rapidly for 10 minutes. Reduce the heat, cover, and let simmer for 15 minutes, or until tender. Meanwhile, preheat the broiler to medium. Spread the pine nuts out in a single layer on a baking sheet and toast under the broiler, turning to brown evenly—watch constantly because they brown quickly. Turn the pine nuts into a small dish and set aside.

2 Heat the oil in a skillet over medium heat, add the onion, garlic, and zucchini and cook, stirring frequently, for 8–10 minutes. Add the tomatoes and artichoke halves and cook for 5 minutes or until heated through. Meanwhile, put the couscous into a heatproof bowl. Bring the stock to a boil in a pan and pour over the couscous, cover, and let stand for 10 minutes, until the couscous absorbs the stock and is tender.

3 Drain the lentils and stir into the couscous. Stir in the torn basil leaves and season well with pepper. Transfer the couscous to a warmed serving dish and spoon over the cooked vegetables. Sprinkle the pine nuts over the top, garnish with basil, and serve at once.

WARM RED LENTIL SALAD WITH GOAT CHEESE

Serves 4

Ingredients

2 tbsp olive oil
2 tsp cumin seeds
2 garlic cloves, crushed
2 tsp grated fresh ginger
1¹/₂ cups split red lentils
3 cups vegetable stock
2 tbsp chopped fresh mint
2 tbsp chopped fresh cilantro
2 red onions, thinly sliced
4¹/₂ cups baby spinach leaves
1 tsp hazelnut oil
5¹/₂ oz/150 g soft goat cheese
4 tbsp strained plain yogurt
pepper
To serve
1 lemon, cut into quarters, to garnish
toasted rye bread

Nutritional Fact

Lentils and spinach contain B vitamins and iron. These are important for energy production and controlling sugar cravings.

Serving Analysis
• Calories 310
• Protein 16 g
• Carbohydrate 24 g
• Sugars 6 g
• Fat 17 g
• Saturates 5.9 g

1 Heat half the olive oil in a large pan over medium heat, add the cumin seeds, garlic, and ginger and cook for 2 minutes, stirring constantly. Stir in the lentils, then add the stock, a ladleful at a time, until it is all absorbed, stirring constantly—this will take about 20 minutes. Remove from the heat and stir in the herbs.

2 Meanwhile, heat the remaining olive oil in a skillet over medium heat, add the onions, and cook, stirring frequently, for 10 minutes, or until soft and lightly browned.

3 Toss the spinach in the oil, then divide between 4 serving plates. Mash the goat cheese with the yogurt and season with pepper to taste.

4 Divide the lentils between the serving plates and top with the onions and goat cheese mixture. Garnish with lemon quarters and serve with toasted rye bread.

BLUEBERRY FROZEN YOGURT

Serves 4

Ingredients
¾ cup fresh blueberries
finely grated rind and juice of 1 orange
3 tbsp maple syrup
2¼ cups plain low-fat yogurt

Nutritional Fact
Blueberries may increase sensitivity to insulin and help to control Type II diabetes.

Serving Analysis
• Calories 157
• Protein 7 g
• Carbohydrate 29 g
• Sugars 26 g
• Fat 2 g
• Saturates 1.1 g

1 Put the blueberries and orange juice into a food processor or blender and process to a puree. Strain through a nylon strainer into a bowl or pitcher.

2 Stir the maple syrup and yogurt together in a large mixing bowl, then fold in the fruit puree.

3 Churn the mixture in an ice-cream machine, following the manufacturer's instructions, then freeze for 5–6 hours. If you don't have an ice-cream machine, transfer the mixture to a freezerproof container, and freeze for 2 hours. Remove from the freezer, turn out into a bowl, and beat until smooth. Return to the freezer and freeze until firm.

LITTLE SEMISWEET CHOCOLATE MOUSSE POTS WITH POACHED BERRIES

Serves 4

Ingredients

$3^{1}/_{2}$ oz/100 g semisweet chocolate, minimum 70% cocoa solids
2 tbsp unsalted butter
2 eggs, separated
1 tbsp maple syrup
scant $^{1}/_{2}$ cup mixed dark berries, such as blackberries, blackcurrants, and blueberries
1 tbsp crème de cassis
fresh mint leaves, to decorate

Nutritional Fact

Semisweet chocolate is lower in sugar than milk chocolate and can be an occasional treat if eaten in small amounts, such as in this recipe.

Serving Analysis
• Calories 241
• Protein 4.4 g
• Carbohydrate 24 g
• Sugars 20 g
• Fat 16 g
• Saturates 8.7 g

1 Break the chocolate into pieces, put into a heatproof bowl with the butter, and place over a pan of simmering water. Let melt, then let cool slightly. Stir in the egg yolks and maple syrup.

2 Whisk the egg whites in a large bowl until stiff, then fold into the cooled chocolate mixture. Divide between 4 ramekins and let chill in the refrigerator for 3 hours.

3 Meanwhile, put the berries into a small pan with the crème de cassis over low heat, and cook for 5–10 minutes, or until the berries are glossy and soft. Let cool.

4 To serve, spoon the berries on top of the chocolate mousse and decorate with mint leaves.

INDEX

NOTES

....

....

....

....

....

....

....

....

....

....

....

....